SOMEONE is WATCHING...

and waiting.

SOMEONE is WATCHING...

and waiting.

CHRISTINA FRENCH

SOMEONE IS WATCHING... AND WAITING.

iUniverse books may be ordered through booksellers or by contacting:

iUniverse
1663 Liberty Drive
Bloomington, IN 47403
www.iuniverse.com
1-800-Authors (1-800-288-4677)

ISBN: 978-1-5320-4925-5 (sc)
ISBN: 978-1-5320-4926-2 (e)

Print information available on the last page.

iUniverse rev. date: 05/09/2018

CONTENTS

PREFACE

There are many types of predators or stalkers, if you will, and many degrees of predation. From the anonymous phone caller who may or may not ever make himself visible to his victim; to the sudden accosting of and taking advantage of a situation. There is the careful planning and perpetration of a crime. There is the stalker who lies in wait and finally reveals his presence, and the more intent, indeed more dangerous one who lurks and waits and hopes to eventually assault, rob and/or murder his victim. Sometimes this lurking is only of short duration. Sometimes it is more lengthy and involved.

Now we come to the labels we can attach to these deviants: Dangerous, Insane, Pervert Predator, Psychologically Disturbed, Sinister, Stalker

These predators existed long before the advent of computer dating but now it is far easier for a person with mercenary and/or evil goals to initiate, develop and pursue that intent to its end, if they choose that route. But there are many other routes to take. For the purpose of writing this book I'll deal only with men whom I have encountered in real, everyday life and not with the relatively newer technique found on dating sites.

Example:

You are visiting in a foreign country. Very early in the morning you are awakened by a strange male voice coming from the adjoining room, speaking in Spanish. Your TV is on. You look at your watch. It is1:30 a.m. Thinking that perhaps the sound is disturbing the occupants in the adjoining room. you turn the volume down. You can see light coming from under the adjoining door. Drowsily you listen for a few minutes, understanding with your somewhat limited command of Spanish, only part of what you hear. Suddenly the conversation turns to a description of your group, the one you are traveling with. "Whetta" is you! "Abuelo"(grandfather), is Ricardo, your host, who looks much older than his wife Rosa. There is a mention of their 5 year-old daughter and the two other friends you are traveling with. The voice goes on to ask a question: Has he checked the adjoining door from their room to yours? You hear a guttural male voice tell him it is locked.

The stories in this book are all true accounts of incidents, as told from firsthand knowledge of this author.

Most of these stories made me know that one needs to be aware at all times. Take precautions, remain skeptical while trying to keep a healthy attitude. Make sure your doors and windows are securely locked. Don't go into remote places unprotected. Always make sure you won't run out of gas in dangerous and even seemingly non-dangerous places. Believe that sometimes even the most innocent-looking and innocent-sounding persons and situations can have strange, if not evil, intent and consequences.

The true stories in this book began several decades ago and are still happening up to the present time. All but one are personal accounts.

1

JAIL CELL JAILBAIT

I was fourteen years old and in a Kansas jail cell for stealing a car. The judge had sent me and my friend Dorothy there while he could decide what our punishment was going to be. The women's side of the second-story jail consisted of a large outer cell with two bunk beds, sort of like a dormitory. Off to the side of this larger cell were three small, regular-sized cells, cages, if you will.

Soon after being incarcerated I discovered that there were prisoners on the men's side that we could talk with through the heating grate which connected one of our small cells to one of theirs. If we bent down and peered through the grate we could see each other. They could also pass cigarettes to us, via a nail on a stick or broom handle, probably supplied by a bribed trustee. I had some pretty steamy, suggestive conversations with one of the inmates. It was probably the one being held on a rape charge. I'll call him No Name. I knew it wasn't the town idiot, Jimmy, who was an inmate too, (and proud of it) because I knew what he looked and sounded like. In one of these conversations No Name told me in no uncertain terms what he would do to me if we ever got together. I didn't think that would ever happen.

The next morning I heard the clanging of the outer jail cell door, It was too early for breakfast. When I looked out of the small cell where I had slept the night before, I saw the trustee.

He said, "There's somebody here to see you."

Behind him stood, I assumed, No Name, the prisoner I'd been talking to the night before. He appeared to be very excited.

I said, "Well, I don't want to see him!" I pulled the door shut on my cell, locking me in and anyone else, including No Name, out. The trustee and his briber benefactor quickly disappeared.

When the guard appeared with the breakfast tray he asked me why the cell door was closed. I answered, a little too smart-alecky probably, that I just wanted some privacy, He said sarcastically, "Okay, you can have all the privacy you want. Just stay in there for a while and cool your heels."

Nothing came from my near encounter with the convict but about three months later the 40 year-old sentencing judge came to the small neighboring town where I had been exiled to live with my aunt, with the hope for me to be rehabilitated. The probate judge told my aunt he wanted to talk to me in private.

On that quiet, late Saturday morning in June he drove to a nearby park. There was nobody around. He talked of inconsequential things. He said he was happy to learn that I was going to be the acrobatic twirler in the band and that it pleased him that I was doing so well in my studies.

Then he put his arms around me. I didn't move. I didn't act as if I'd even noticed his move. Fleetingly I wondered if this might just be a fatherly gesture. I quickly dismissed that thought. I knew what it was. I remained frozen. The judge continued talking soothingly and, seeing no response from me, he took his arms away.

Then he took me back to my aunt's house and told her I

was ready to go home. I would be on probation for two years and I would have to report to him, the supposedly highly respectable judge, every week.

Who knows what would have happened if I had shown any acceptance of his advances or if in the ensuing months he tried it again?

I was very sorry for the crime that I had committed. I realized what my actions had done to others. I never would have stolen again. But I was still defiant in my attitude about most things because of our extreme poverty and the inequality of life as I perceived it and I showed my resentment when I had to visit the court on my weekly obligatory visits to the judge. I was insolent and noncommittal. The court psychiatrist told me I had to want help before they could give it.

I ended up getting married eight months later. Since I was now a ward of the court, I had to ask the judge's permission. He didn't hesitate in giving it to me, he was probably glad to be rid of me. No more temptation. Or maybe he had found a more willing target.

Many years later I learned from a friend of mine, Bonnie, who lived in my hometown, that her mother had told her years before that the judge was disbarred and run out of town because of his improprieties with young girls.

2

Re-Up

Frank

I was fourteen years old and went to the dances with my friends Rosie and Bonnie at a high school auditorium in a town 20 miles away. That's where I met Frank. He told me he was a soldier, stationed about 75 miles away. I danced with him a few times. He was a pretty good dancer and I could tell he liked me but I wasn't overly impressed with him. So when he asked if he could take me home I told him I didn't think so. Later when I was talking to Rosie she said that we should go with them because she really liked Artie. He was the driver that night for Frank. So I went over to Frank and told him that I guessed we would go home with them. Bonnie went home with her brother. On the way home I had to fend off Frank's panting and pawing. Finally I told him to behave or I'd get out and walk. He straightened up, shook his head and said he'd behave.

"But I'm just crazy about you girl!"

When they took me home he asked if we'd go out with them the next day, Sunday. He said, "Yeah, we've got until tomorrow night to get back to the post."

I agreed after I saw Rosie nodding her head in the front seat.

We dated for about two weeks. Then Frank told me that he was going to "re-up", or in layman's terms, re-enlist. He said that he would get some money that way and maybe he could get a car so we wouldn't have to ride with his friends all the time. I didn't like what this sounded like and besides I'd begun to grow tired of Frank and his constant pawing.

"Well, don't do anything on my account!" I told him.

It had been about six weeks since I'd last seen Frank at the dance. Bonnie, Rosie, and her brother and I went there Saturday night. I was wearing my ice blue, silk, sleeveless blouse that I thought made my blue eyes look pretty, especially with my dyed long black hair.

Soon after we got there, I was standing over at the side of the dance floor when Frank came walking up to me.

"I was hoping you'd be here," he grinned at me. "Come outside with me, I want to show you something."

I protested, saying that I'd just barely gotten there, but he insisted.

We walked outside and across the parking lot in the dusk with Frank beaming the whole time.

"You know I re-enlisted right? Well this is what I bought," he said as he put his hand on a shiny car that was parked there. "Now we won't have to ride with my buddies all the time. We can be alone." He opened the car door. "Come on, let's go for a ride."

"No, I don't want to go for a ride," I said, and started to turn around to go back into the building.

"C'mon! I did this for you," Frank yelled. "For us!" He grabbed my arm.

"I told you not to do it for me!" I snapped back as I jerked

5

away from him and continued walking across the lot to the building.

I didn't hear the car's motor starting up or notice the headlights until I looked over my shoulder and saw that it was almost upon me. I jumped aside. The car crashed into the brick building. I was afraid of what Frank might do so I rushed into the building and frantically looked around for Bonnie.

"Frank tried to kill me!" I gasped.

People had heard the crash and were rushing out the door. Rosie's brother saw that I was shaken and he came over to me as Bonnie was calling to Rosie to come on. We left the dance. I never saw or heard from Frank again.

3

VISITOR IN THE MORNING

I was excited when Sharon called me and asked me to go to Oklahoma with her and her dad. I would get to go out of town, even if it did mean that I would be away for Christmas. I wouldn't come back until New Year's Day. But that was okay with me. The holidays weren't very exciting at my house. There was never much money to do anything and no tradition to worry about, like some other families had. I just hoped that my mother would agree to let me go.

Sharon was my best friend and she had moved away from our town the summer before, when her dad's road-building job took him out of Kansas and to a little town in western Oklahoma. Sharon lived a nomadic existence, since her alcoholic mother had died several years before. They traveled from town to town, her dad going wherever his job of driving a big Caterpillar took him. They rented rooms or apartments and Sharon usually had to shift for herself. Her dad drank a lot and Sharon had told me that sometimes he was passed–out drunk.

She said that a couple of weeks before, her dad had asked her what she wanted for Christmas and she had told him she'd like to go to Kansas, pick me up and take me down to see Oklahoma and New Mexico. Her dad had agreed.

Saturday night Sharon and I drove in Ike's new Buick, to a little town across the border into New Mexico. We got to The nightclub right at 8:00 o'clock, when the dance was just beginning. Inside, Sharon was looking around and spied the one she was looking for. A good looking, Spanish or Indian guy came right over to us. He hugged Sharon and said Hi to me when Sharon introduced us. Tony called Sharon "Carmen" and I remembered that she told everybody to call her by that name. They started dancing right away. I sat and watched for a while until a guy came over to me and then it was non-stop dancing until closing time. Tony told us as we were leaving, that we should come to the New Year's Eve party on Monday night. Sharon told him we would.

It was pretty late when we got home. Sharon noted that her dad's company truck wasn't in its usual parking spot. He let Sharon drive the Buick whenever she wanted to and he used the truck to take him to his work site or out on the town.

"He probably went to town to drink with some of his friends. That's usually what he does on Saturday night. He probably won't come home until morning. I think you should sleep in his bed and I'll stay in mine—that way we can both stretch out."

I was asleep and it was still dark in the bedroom when I was wakened by hands touching me and then sliding over my body. I opened my eyes and in the pale light that was creeping around the edges of the window shades, I could see Ike sitting at the edge of the bed, bending over me. He was cooing softly to me.

"Oh you sweet little thing. Shh, don't be afraid. I won't hurt you." He was slurring his words. I started to cry a little. I tried to push his hands away.

"Oh, honey, I just can't help myself. I see you running around in your tight little pants and I just want you so bad . . ."

Just then the door burst open and Sharon was screaming at him, "You son-of-a-bitch! Get your hands off her!" She pulled at his arms.

Ike dropped his hands and whimpered, "I didn't hurt her. Christina, you tell Sharon I didn't hurt you."

I said, sniffling, "No, he didn't hurt me."

Ike got up and left the room. Sharon hugged me. She said, "Honey, I am so sorry. I can't believe he did that."

She told me later that day that her dad wasn't going to bother me any more, that she had had a talk with him and I probably wouldn't have to see any more of him. He was going to keep to himself. That day, Sunday, I didn't know if Ike was even around. He wasn't there for supper. And the next day, we were going to go to the New Year's Eve party. I would have to leave early Tuesday morning to be driven to the bus station in Liberal, Kansas by a driver and then I would catch the bus there to travel the 300 miles to my hometown. Ike had left my bus ticket on his dresser.

Sharon and I never spoke of the incident again. She and I are still good friends but Sharon's memory of most things is gone. She has forgotten this, I am sure. Thankfully. But my memory still holds on to details.

4

MILLION DOLLAR BABY IN THE FIVE AND TEN CENT STORE

I realize that you can't always be prepared for some things. Like the time an unwanted pursuer had followed me home from work.

I was working at a five and ten cent store in Pittsburgh. I was sixteen. I was married. I was also very friendly and talkative, especially at work. I had gotten married six months before in Kansas and shortly thereafter we had moved to my husband's hometown, which I found to be very clannish at first. I had no friends so I went out of my way to be friendly. At work I would talk to anyone who seemed to want to have a conversation.

One morning a nice-looking, impressively dressed man stood at my stationery counter, engaging me in small talk which eventually led to his asking me if I was single. I told him no, that I had gotten married not too many months before. Soon he went on his way.

When I left work at 5:00 p.m., heading home to our second floor apartment which was seven long blocks away, I walked four blocks to the supermarket where I bought some pork chops for our dinner. From there I crossed the street to look in the window of the pet store, I watched the birds and small animals in their cages and then I continued on for two blocks. Then I crossed back over busy Highland Avenue and on up the street. Soon I reached the two flights of concrete steps which would take me up to the apartment house. Once inside the door I had another flight of steps to climb, up to the second floor and then a long hallway before I reached the door to my apartment. My husband was there already and I got out my pots and pans to begin cooking.

"How was your day?" my husband asked.

I told him we had been pretty busy and that I had talked with several customers and one of the men had acted a little too friendly, maybe, asking me if I was married. I had told him yes.

"You shouldn't talk to people so much. You're too damned friendly!"

Just then there was a knock on our door. I opened it and the man from that morning was standing there, grinning at me.

"Oh!" I was shocked.

Then his gaze left my face and traveled over my shoulder to where my husband stood.

"This is my husband."

"Oh, so you were married," he mumbled as he scurried away down the hall.

"Maybe that'll teach you not to be so friendly all the time!" my husband growled.

The man had to have been determined though, because of the distance I lived from the store where I worked, across busy city streets and then the stops I had made. Had he followed me through the supermarket? Or had he lurked outside, waiting for me to come out? Was he watching me as I watched the birds and hamsters in their cages? Where was he when I walked up the considerable steps to the apartment building and then up still more steps? How did he know which apartment I lived in? How had he done all that without my seeing him? I suspected nothing.

Question: What would have happened if my husband hadn't been in the apartment?

5

ANONYMOUS TELEPHONE CALLER

When my first child was a few months old my husband found a house to rent that was in a different part of Pittsburgh, several miles from the third floor apartment where we lived in the house of my friend Lucy. I looked at Lucy as my adopted mother since my own mother lived a thousand miles away. I felt safe in her house. I knew no one in this new place, other than the family next door. They had two daughters close to my age which was seventeen. But I had a three month old daughter.

Two months after moving in the phone calls started. My husband would leave in the early morning and the phone would ring shortly after he was gone. I would answer and a stranger with a slightly familiar voice would talk to me in a soft, sweet, sing-song voice. After asking who it was several times I would hang up. Then a couple of mornings later the phone would ring.

"Did you miss me? I just want to talk to you."

I would never say anything to encourage him. I'd just hang up.

Then his conversation became more personal, saying things like he wanted to "gently spank" me and asking if my husband ever spanked me. There was nothing obscene, just the obscenity of his sickeningly sweet mutterings and their implications. And the fact that he knew precisely the right moment to call, always after my husband had gone to work. He never called when my husband was home. That caused me to wonder if it was somebody who lived close by who watched our movements, like the teenaged boy up the street, but I dismissed him because I wondered how he would have known our phone number. Or possibly it was our Italian neighbor, the father of my friends Penny and Veronica next door. Or maybe it was somebody who knew us and our habits, like one of my husband's friends. I never found out.

6

THE SCREEN DOOR

I n the next place we lived there was the incident of the squeaking screen door. This happened when we were living in a duplex on a suburban road outside Pittsburgh, with houses on our side of the road only. This was mountainous country with many houses built on hillsides. Ours was like that, with an extremely steep, treed slope behind our duplex.

One evening I had had a small party with a Hawaiian theme. After the few neighbors and friends had left and my husband had gone into the neighborhood bar to have a few drinks, I was clearing the dishes and rinsing them off in the kitchen sink, which was immediately by the back door. It had a screen door with a flimsy, little hook lock, which was always hooked. But in spite of this, because it was loose, the screen door made a scraping sound when pushed or pulled.

I hadn't turned on the kitchen light, relying on the light coming from the adjacent dining room to see to rinse the dishes. There was no curtain on the window of the door, only a narrow valance at the top. I had just gotten the last of the remnants from the party and carried the cake to the counter, and set it down. I rinsed the cake knife in running water.

Then I heard the scrape of the screen door.

Alarmed, I looked up to my left and saw a white T-shirt first and then the face above it. He was watching me. I turned away and returned to the dining room area, where the telephone was. Quickly I dialed my neighbor Sally, who lived in the adjoining duplex.

"Hi Chris! Great party . .," Sally began.

"Sally! Somebody's trying to get in my back door!"

"What? Chris, stay calm!"

I could hear Sally saying something to her husband Dan.

"Chris, Dan's got a gun and he's coming right over. Let him in the front door."

Dan came rushing in with Sally close behind him, telling me that she had called the police. "They should be here soon."

"What happened?" Dan asked, looking shocked.

I explained to him, while he listened intently. He looked out the back door but he didn't attempt to go outside.

When the cops arrived, I told my story again. They asked for a description. The best I could do was that he had dark hair, wore a white T-shirt and was probably my height, which was five foot seven inches, or a little taller,

After conducting a search, the police informed me that there had been a robbery on the hill above where our duplex was and their thoughts were that the robber had fled down the hillside in an attempt to get away. Possibly he was going to cut through my house or hide out there for a while. Or maybe rob me too.

I never found out any more about it.

What if my neighbor hadn't been at home?

7

CHRISTMAS COOKIES

A s was the custom with a lot of young, married women, we shared Christmas cookie baking. It was an economical way of getting a large variety of cookies and having your girlfriends share the baking was more fun than if you were doing it on your own. This year, I was going to bake with my friend Pat, who lived in an isolated farmhouse at the juncture of a brick street which turned into a steep road. This meandered along a heavily wooded hillside, a mile-long, narrow roadway which was devoid of houses and on down to join up with a major thoroughfare. This was a neighborhood in Pittsburgh which was nearly all black. Pittsburgh was not too well-integrated at that time and my very bigoted husband had warned me not to go into this area, saying that it wasn't safe. But my desire for an abundance of cookies for my family's Christmas outweighed his admonitions and I probably didn't believe his theory about this being unsafe anyway since I always ignored his racial slurs, so I set out in the little stick-shift Ford which was good in the snow and now there was an abundance of that on the ground.

The major roads were pretty well cleared but the side streets could be slippery. This car had a tricky ignition which was loose. If you didn't watch when you inserted the key, the whole thing would push in and have to be pried out, but I had learned how to coax it and wiggle it and I was careful, as a rule, not to push it in.

Pat's husband was in the hospital, recovering from back surgery. Pat had two kids. She had a gun. She felt this was necessary, given the fact that her husband was gone a lot and she was in a location which had no neighbors within hearing distance of her house. The nearest neighbor was about two blocks away, as the crow flies, but you had to navigate a dirt road that led out of her house for about 600 feet to a paved road. Across from this was a cemetery which had locked gates after dark, barring any entrance. From the paved road it was another 100 feet to reach the brick street. Then up a very steep brick street to the top of a hill.

When I traveled the three miles to get from my house to Pat's on this night five days before Christmas, I noted that there was a lot of snow on the road. When I got to the avenue and turned to go up the slight incline to the top of the hill, I knew that I would have to park the car at the bottom of the hill, on the brick street, before I reached Pat's house, because Pat had told me she hadn't had her long, dirt road plowed. It was slippery, going down the brick street but not so much so that I was worried. I passed the houses, most of which had Christmas decorations and lights. Reaching the end of the brick street, I turned my car around so that it would be pointing up the hill.

I figured I would probably be in Pat's house for a couple of hours. It was now eight-thirty. I carried the two shopping bags loaded with my contributions for baking, and cookie sheets and a big canister in which to pack the cookies.

The baking took longer than either of us had thought it

would. It was well past eleven when I started loading up the unused ingredients. Pat and I divided up the cookies.

"Well, I'd better hurry home," I said as I buttoned my coat and wrapped the wool scarf around my head. I hadn't worn gloves so my hands were sure to get cold.

"I'll watch you out the window," Pat told me. "You call me when you get home, okay?"

I told her I would. I headed out, carrying my two shopping bags, filled with supplies and the big potato chip canister which held the Christmas cookies.

It was tough-going on the snowy road, even when you weren't loaded down with shopping bags filled with flour, sugar, baking sheets and cookies resting in their canister. My boots weren't very good so I had to take special care not to slip. I had gone about a third of the way on the dirt road by an open field when Pat called out to me.

"Are you okay?"

I glanced back over my shoulder. I could see Pat at her upstairs open window. I called back to her, "Yes, I'm okay."

I would soon come abreast of the fork in the road where to the left went down the steep and winding narrow road, to meet the highway a mile distant. A right turn would put me on the short stretch of paved narrow road before it connected to the slippery brick street. Directly across from the fork was the cemetery. It was now approaching midnight and getting very cold. I wished that there were more street lights.

Pat called out again, "You okay, Chris?"

"Yeah, I'm okay. Kinda cold," I yelled back.

Soon I was at the juncture which was directly across from the lane that led up a slight incline to the gates of the cemetery. I could look ahead and see the gates now. There was a car parked there. I didn't remember seeing the car when I had arrived at Pat's earlier. Then I saw a figure . . . a very large man emerging from the shadows behind the car. He was wearing a topcoat.

Pat called out a third time. Her voice was faint now. "Are you okay?"

I chose not to answer this time. I didn't want to call attention to myself in case the man hadn't seen me. I was out of Pat's sight now, having gone behind a row of trees which were devoid of leaves now that it was winter but they still obscured my presence from Pat. She would have shut her window by now. I could see that the rows of houses on either side of the street had turned off their Christmas lights. I tried not to feel alarmed but I quickened my steps, which was not easy to do on this now much more slippery paved road and with my arms loaded. I couldn't afford to lose my balance now.

Suddenly, "Is there a phone around here?", the man in the topcoat bellowed out to me in a deep, gruff voice.

I pretended not to hear him. I tried to move faster. I could see that he was starting to move away from the car, down the slight incline, the incline which would soon join up with my path. I tried to go faster. I must not panic.

"I said, 'Is there a phone down here?'", "he yelled again, louder now. But no one was within earshot of him, only me. And I didn't know if I had to scream, if anyone would hear me or if they did hear, if they would go out of their house at midnight to help me.

I had almost reached the car. I didn't turn around to see where the man was. I fished the keys out of my pocket and wiggled my hand around the handles on the bag and unlocked the door. I jerked the door open, threw the bags into the car and hopped in, slamming down on the door lock as soon as I could. Hurriedly I inserted the key. The ignition receptacle sank in. I felt despair begin to grip me.

Keep your head, I told myself, as I gently pried it back

out. I didn't dare look to see where the man was. I started the engine, put the car in gear and started up the incline but the wheels were spinning on the slick bricks. I would have to back up to the level part and get a run at the hill. I backed down and began the climb and as I did I passed the hulk who was standing in the middle of the road where the driver's door of my car had been seconds before. He must have been right behind me as I reached my car.

When I arrived at my home I had gripped the steering wheel so tightly while driving that my fingernails had dug grooves into the palms of my hands.

My husband wasn't very sympathetic. "I told you not to go there."

Why was the man there? Differing theories were that he was drunk and had driven down there, after leaving a bar, or friends' house in the area, that his car had broken down and he really was looking for a phone. Or that he was high on drugs, that he was robbing the car or trying to, when I approached and then thought that he would rob me or do something else. Questions remained:

1. Why was he on a deserted lane by the cemetery at midnight?
2. Why not go to one of the houses if he was really looking for a phone?
3. Why try to catch up with me?
4. What would he have done if he had been a little faster or I had been a little slower?

8

AT THE WINDOW

I t seemed each new house brought new experiences with predators.

The next house was the only house on a busy street with a lot of businesses, all of which were closed at six o'clock or thereabouts. My husband had chosen this house because of its proximity to a building which housed the transmission business which my husband and his partner ran. Its front door was about thirty feet from our back door. The nearest neighbor was over a block away.

One night my husband had gone into the Avenue to meet and greet his buddies. After putting my three kids to bed, I had watched a little TV and then decided to take a bath before going to bed.

The bathroom adjoined my bedroom and was situated between mine and that of my children. I went in to run the water for the tub. I had started to undress as the tub filled and I dropped my bra on the floor of the bathroom. I bent down to pick it up and as I raised back up my eyes naturally traveled upward to the top of the tall window. The bottom half was frosted glass but the top wasn't. It was clear glass and there was a face watching me.

SOMEONE IS WATCHING... AND WAITING.

I didn't let on that I had seen anything. I turned the water off and went back through my bedroom and on out to the breakfast room, where there was a telephone. I dialed my friend Loretta, who lived just a few blocks away.

"Loretta! Call the police! There's a man outside my house, watching me!"

I peered out the window on the opposite side of the house of where the predator had been.

"Stay calm, I'll call for help!"

It didn't take long before I saw a patrol car swing into the driveway. Loretta's car followed close behind. She jumped out and came rushing into the house.

"Are you all right?" Loretta was out of breath and visibly frightened.

"Yes, Loretta. I'm okay. Thanks for coming."

One of the cops began taking my statement while another one was outside, shining his flashlight along the hedges. Then I could see the flashlight's beam going over to the side yard and back around the garage area. There weren't too many places he could hide. After a few minutes the officer came in to give his report.

"Well, he's gone. I saw how he was able to look in that high window though. You've got that picnic table out there, right? With the benches attached?"

I nodded my head.

"Well," the cop sighed, "he just slid it over a couple of feet so he could stand up on the table. He had a clear shot looking down into the bathroom."

I wondered who it was or how he had known to go into the back yard?

"We'll keep looking for him but we've got an idea who it was. A patient escaped from the mental hospital about a week ago. It's just up the road. This sounds like something he might

23

do. Up 'til now all that we know for sure that he did was steal some ladies' panties off a clothesline. The lady saw him but he ran off while she was yelling for him to stop."

Question: Would a mental patient have had the mental wherewithal to know to move the picnic table? How had he gotten into the fenced yard? Did he jump the fence? Did he know that there would be something to look at? If so, how did he know?

9

THE ALIEN

After I had divorced my first husband and was living in California, in a farmhouse with my three daughters, and my boyfriend, an illegal broke in and took refuge under my daughter's bed one day during a storm. This was the last week in August. We had all learned to lock every door. Only one problem: the back door had no lock. Its screen door had a flimsy hook lock but you could only lock it when you were inside. I had intended to fix it but hadn't gotten around to it yet. After all there was hardly any traffic on the road of this rural farmhouse nor any passers-by.

It had one passer-by on this day in late August. The young fugitive had probably made it across the Mexican border, which was only one to two miles distant from the farmhouse, depending upon where he crossed or cut or climbed the fence, possibly during the night or early morning. He had probably passed by other homes, which were in the area, although there were few and none really close by. Perhaps he had seen activity in those and continued on.

Seeing no signs of life at this house during several minutes of observation from the various fields all around it, he decided to approach the door. He knocked. There was no answer. He could have peered in the windows, which covered one whole wall at the front of the house but this could be seen if a car should pass by on the road out front. I refused to drape these, preferring to allow the light to fill the room. He couldn't have seen beyond this room however, which held nothing but bookcases, so it's more likely that he would have made his way around the house and knocked at the back door. Hearing nothing he concluded that the house was empty.

He entered the house, anticipating an encounter at every step. He did find one live thing in the house: a small white dog. It barked and growled at him. It was in the bedroom which had a blue rug on the floor. He merely pulled the door shut and continued inspecting the house. Finding nothing more to impede his progress, he made his plans for a later departure, after darkness fell. He raised the window in the dining room and unhooked the screen. He left the window raised about an inch. He took off his shoes and carried them and the small bundle of clothes that he had brought, outside to place them under a palm tree in the side yard. He went back into the house and opened the refrigerator. He took two slices of the bologna he found and spying a loaf of bread on the counter, he made himself a sandwich. Then releasing a banana from the bunch that sat there, he continued on his rounds of the house, tossing the peel on the dining room table. There were some decanters sitting on a buffet in the dining room. He pulled the stopper out of one and took a swig but quickly spat it out. These were decorative decanters which I had filled with water with food coloring added to them. Now he would choose his hiding place, where he would wait for night to fall so he could make his getaway. He chose one of the twin beds in the room, which Theresa and Kim shared.

When Kim came home to an empty house, (at least devoid of her family), at four o'clock in the afternoon, she found Gigi, the toy poodle, in Denise's room, with the door shut. Denise was in Pittsburgh, not due home for a week. Kim thought that possibly her mother, me, had put Gigi there before leaving to take her other sister, Theresa, to spend a few days with her friend in Canoga Park. She thought perhaps I just hadn't noticed Gigi when I had left the house that morning. Kim didn't think any more about it.

She looked under the bed and in the closet, as she always did and continued into the other bedroom, where she looked under the twin bed that was hers and in the closet. Just then the phone rang and she went out to the kitchen to answer it. It was her friend Julie, calling her to make sure she'd gotten home all right and to tell her that a storm was expected to bring a lot of rain that evening. In fact it had already started to rain lightly. As they spoke, Kim noticed that some things were out of place, like the wine decanter in the dining room and the bologna sitting on the counter in the kitchen. I had been the last one to leave that morning and those things shouldn't have been out of place. Well, she told herself, maybe Larry, my boyfriend, had come home and grabbed a fast sandwich and forgot to put it back. A banana peel on the table? That was strange.

She went about doing what she normally did, watching TV and talking on the phone with her friends.

For four hours twelve-year old Kim was alone in the house with Gigi, and the alien under Theresa's bed in the other room. A steady rain fell outside.

Larry came home from work a little after 8:00 o'clock and talked with Kim for a while and then announced that he was tired and was going upstairs to lie down and listen to the radio.

Ordinarily Kim slept on the couch, preferring it to the shared bedroom but tonight she thought it would be cozier to sleep in her own twin bed. Then too, Theresa had gone out of town so she'd have the room all to herself. Gigi followed her as she went into the bedroom to get her white, flimsy nightgown. She slipped out of her shirt and Levi's. After unhooking her bra she let the soft gown fall over her shoulders. She noticed that Gigi was sniffing at her bed, the only one that she had failed to check when she was interrupted by the ringing of the telephone.

"What's the matter, Gigi? Is Blanca under there?" Thinking that one of their many cats had gotten in and was under the bed, she knelt down on the floor and whipped up the bedspread. Peering under, she saw brown stocking- covered feet. Someone had Levi's on the legs above the feet.

Kim was confused. Was this Theresa, her sister, playing a trick on her? Something wasn't right. She began to feel fear creeping over her. She hurriedly straightened up and headed for the steps that led to the second floor where Larry slept. Her legs wouldn't take her as fast as she wanted to go.

She tried to go up the steps. She called out, "Larry, can you come down here?"

His voice answered groggily, "Huh? What's the matter?"

Her legs wouldn't move. She yelled, "Somebody's under the bed!"

She turned, just as the dark-haired man came towards her and reached the end of the hallway which led to the foot of the stairs. She stood 10 feet away from the alien who had dark, bushy hair and a heavy mustache. He was wearing a white T-shirt and Levi's. Fear gripped her. She tried to scream and couldn't. Her legs felt like rubber bands and wouldn't move. She wanted to get out of the reach of this man but just then he swept past her and through the kitchen and bounded out the door. Larry had stormed out of his room and down the steps and nearly crashed into Kim who was frozen in shock.

SOMEONE IS WATCHING... AND WAITING.

"Larry, where are you going? Don't leave me!" Kim was shaking now.

"I'll get the bastard," he yelled as he searched for a weapon of some sort. All he could find was a spatula.

"No! What if he kills you?" Kim cried, her voice filled with panic.

But the stranger was in a hurry to get out of there. Having flung open the kitchen door, he burst through the screen door, breaking the hook lock, and continued his flight through the fields which had gotten quite muddy with all the rain that had been falling steadily.

When I, Kim's mother, returned from the 400 mile round-trip at two o'clock in the morning, border patrol lights were sweeping the fields and men were dragging tires through them, in search of the intruder. He got away but not without leaving his mark. All of my daughters had nightmares for a long time after that.

Hence another lesson learned was to always fix those locks, hide a key for emergencies, check under all beds and in all suspicious places and pay attention to your intuition.

But what if Kim had been alone in the house with no Larry? I'll always believe that the alien could hear the voices of the TV set and Kim talking on the phone. Maybe he thought there was more than one person in the house and that he should just wait under the bed until everything was quiet and then make his escape. But what if Kim had raised the bedspread on Theresa's bed when she was alone in the house? Alone with the alien.

10

STOLEN IN THE NIGHT

The setting was an affluent section around San Diego, beautiful Mt. Helix.

Lexie was asleep in her bed. She was seven years old. Her older sister, Jen was babysitting her while my good friend Fran, their mother, was out for the evening with friends. It was Saturday night in San Diego.

When Fran returned home in the early morning hours, she went first to Lexie's bedroom to tuck her in. She wasn't there. The bed was empty. Fran thought she must have gone to Jen's room. Then Fran turned and headed down the hall to her older daughter's bedroom. Lexie wasn't there either. Jen was sleeping soundly on her side.

Thinking that perhaps her daughter had gone into the bathroom, Fran crossed the few steps and opened the door but the bathroom was empty. Confused she went back to the bedroom and noticed that Lexie's blanket was missing This was strange. Lexie always slept with that blanket. Had Lexie fallen onto the floor? Peering down and sweeping her arm under the bed told Fran that Lexie was not in the room. She hurried back to Fran's room and shook her awake.

SOMEONE IS WATCHING... AND WAITING.

"Where's Lexie?" Fran demanded of her 16 year old daughter.

Jen rubbed her eyes. "Huh?"

"Lexie's not in her bed! C'mon, help me look for her."

My good friend Fran told me this story four years after it happened.

Fran called her ex-husband. They had remained friends after they were divorced. He was alarmed. No, he had no idea where Lexie might be. No, he had not gone to the home to see his kids. He told Fran he would call the police to report the disappearance. He lived close by and he arrived at Fran's house a little before the police did.

A multitude of questions produced nothing helpful in determining where the seven- year old might be. Jen was questioned as to whether anything suspicious had happened. No. Were there any strangers that she noticed? No. Neighbors were questioned. Nobody knew anything. This was not an area that Lexie could have wandered off without someone seeing her. The terrain was hilly and yards were fenced. Someone would have to have walked down the street in front of the houses. Most of them had barking dogs. The FBI was called.

In the ensuing days radio stations carried the news. Newspapers had the story. A psychic was consulted. She told the parents that she saw Lexie sitting in the dust. She was wearing cowboy boots that were too big for her. She was crying.

On Tuesday a lead in the case turned up when the owners of a mobile home reported that someone had robbed them of a pair of cowboy boots and some food from the fridge, cooked pork chops and cheese and some bread. And some milk. This had happened when the owners were out for the evening. And another report came in from the same area, of a break-in which resulted in the loss of some food and some clothes; a sweater, pants, underwear, belonging to the couple's little six year-old boy.

Alerts were sent out via the TV news that anyone noticing something missing should immediately notify the police.

By Thursday a few more reports came in. One of them disclosed some shredded patches from a blanket. Was this Lexie's blanket? The path seemed to be leading to the Mexican border. They seemed to be traveling at night.

The police questioned Fran as to whether any Mexican citizens or workers such as maids, had been in her employ. Fran told them yes they had had gardeners who were from Mexico. But that had been several months before and now they had new workers who had already been questioned.

On Friday around noon a helicopter which was patrolling the area in search of anything strange, flew over the area about a mile from the Mexican border. The co-pilot looked down and saw something white protruding from bushes on the ground below.

Go down closer!" he cried to the pilot. "I see something!"

As they swooped down closer to the ground, he could see it was a small human leg. Suddenly a man emerged from the cover of bushes. He was pulling a little girl with blonde hair behind him.

"That's them!"

The co-pilot radioed for help and then began to lower himself with the winch. The man on the ground dropped the little girl's hand and ran for all he was worth.

Soon the co-pilot was holding Lexie, telling her she was going to be all right and that her mommy wanted to see her.

Cop cars had surrounded the area and some officers were on the ground pursuing the fleeing man. Soon they had him in custody.

It was determined that the 21-year-old man from Mexico

had worked as a gardener's helper at Fran's house. He was somewhat retarded. He told police that while working in Fran's yard and seeing sweet, little, blonde Lexie playing, he wanted to take her to Mexico and marry her. He had planned her abduction and when the opportunity presented itself he waited until he knew the two girls would be sleeping and sneaked into the home. Lexie knew who he was and wasn't as afraid as she would have been if he'd been a stranger. Perhaps he had candy to give her. She didn't cry out. They traveled at night and slept in the daytime.

Lexie was examined by doctors and psychiatrists. They thought that she had probably not been sexually molested. Nor did she seem to be overly psychologically damaged.

An uplifting aspect to this story is that the helicopter was one that was used by searchers and they were specifically looking for Lexie. Their organization was in danger of being de-funded and so this rescue was highlighted on a TV news program, to show support for the search team.

What if the rescue agency had gone defunct? What if the kidnapper had been a few hours quicker? He was within one mile of the Mexican border.

11

*VERA CRUZ

What would you do if you were visiting in a foreign country and awakened at 1:30 a.m. by a strange. male voice speaking in Spanish. in the adjoining room? Drowsily you listened for a few minutes, understanding only part of what you heard, when suddenly the conversation turned to a description of your group, the one you were traveling with. 'Whetta' was you! 'Abuelo'(grandfather), was Ricardo, your host. The voice went on to ask another person if he had checked the adjoining door from their room to yours. The other male voice told him it was locked.

I was living in California, working as a real estate agent. I had sold several income properties to Ricardo, a very wealthy Mexican from Guadalajara. He was happy with the properties and my management of them. He offered to take me on an extended trip from the airport in Guadalajara, down through Mexico to the "boot" and back up to the airport three weeks later. His friends Juan and Maria, who had introduced me to Ricardo, and Ricardo's much younger wife, Rosa and five-year-old daughter, Little Rosa, would accompany us on the trip.

Juan and I flew from Mexicali to Guadalajara on a Saturday morning and met up with the rest of the group. We began our trip which took us past Mexico City, many small towns and into Oaxaca, where we would spend a few days. Quite often I walked about by myself, investigating, finding things of interest and always taking my big video camera with me. I never felt threatened.

After leaving the sites of Oaxaca and its environs, we traveled to Maria's brother's place farther south. He was a colonel in the Mexican army and lived in a barricaded compound with barbed wire and armed guards. He also had several servants, including a chauffeur, who made our stay a pleasant one. One of our excursions rook us to a beach which was deserted except for some fishermen and two cooks who prepared the catch of the day for us: freshly caught lobsters.

One of our day trips was to a huge two-story, open-air market where we would buy the cheese which the area was famous for. I saw a sign written in Spanish. I asked Maria what it said.

She replied, "Yankee, Go Home!"

Throughout Mexico I stuck out because of my red hair and pale complexion and the fact that I spoke English most of the time. I carried a huge camcorder. I was obviously an American.

Upon leaving this area after a few days we headed for the seaport city of Vera Cruz.

We were late in arriving, having stayed a day longer than we had intended at the army compound. As a result Ricardo had to scramble around to get us accommodations for the night. He was familiar with all of the previous hotels, since he was a businessman and had used the places or had dealings with the proprietors. But this hotel was different, he'd never stayed here before. And it was a busy Friday night.

We checked into the hotel and had our things brought up to our rooms on the third floor. My room was at the end of the hall, directly across from Juan and Maria. Ricardo's room was a few doors down from ours. We agreed that we would meet at 5:00 after we had time to freshen up.

I looked around the room which seemed to be nice enough. There was a door, with a double lock, which I surmised was to an adjoining room to mine. The hotel was built on a square but I was at the end of the hall on the third floor. Three floors below was the indoor swimming pool.

I showered and I hurried to dress in a magenta silk jumpsuit. I wanted to take my RCA camcorder and go exploring the hotel. I went by the check-in desk, the pool area, the lobby, waving and smiling at people as I went. Then it was time to meet up with the others and go to a restaurant that Ricardo had wanted to try out.

After dinner we went strolling along the walkway by the ocean. By the time we were finished with that it was getting a little late but I offered to get a nightcap for everyone at the rooftop restaurant in our hotel. I had seen this advertised in the elevator and they boasted of good music.

I was filming all of these activities as we went. Our group looked like prosperous, nicely dressed tourists. And I had a video camera which was a novelty in those days. I'd gotten mine only a few months before and I shot videos everywhere I went. In Mexico I'm sure I was quite a site, bouncing around with my red hair, which was a novelty there and enthusiastically photographing everything.

After listening to the music we said goodnight to Ricardo and his wife and daughter at the door of their room. Juan, Maria and I continued on to our rooms. We had all agreed to meet at 8:00 a.m. the next morning, to check out of the hotel and go to breakfast.

It was a little after midnight. In my room I turned on the TV. It was showing an old movie with subtitles. I put my pajamas on and lay down to watch the movie. I fell asleep quickly.

Voices woke me. I watched a little of the movie and then I realized that the voices were coming from the adjoining room. Thinking that the noise from my set might be disturbing the neighbors, I turned the volume down. I started to drift off to sleep again when I heard a man speaking to someone and he said "Whetta." I knew that this was a word used for a "gringa" or a light-skinned woman. There weren't many of these in Vera Cruz and certainly not in this hotel.

I sat up in bed. Wide awake now, I listened.

The man speaking had a very pleasant voice, soothing and with an accent that sounded like one of Maria's sons who had been educated in Europe. He seemed to be instructing someone in something. My Spanish was only about 50/50, so I missed a lot of what he was saying. I did understand when the voice turned to describe our party; "abuelo" (grandfather, Ricardo) "whetta" (me), younger woman and child (Ricardo's much younger wife and their daughter). Then he asked if the lock on the adjoining door was locked. The other voice told him yes.

All the while there was the sound of water running in their bathroom and someone taking a shower

Then I could hear something that sounded like the shuffling of huge, heavy cardboard cards. Then the sound of a metal box being opened. Then a man's grunt or groan like he'd been punched. Then the pleasant voice said, in Spanish, "Esta bien?" which I interpreted as, "Are you okay?" The other person grunted. All was quiet for a while. Then there was a third person in the room and the pleasant voice was asking if they would have a problem if they had to hurt people—a woman or a child. The answer was "No."

A second grunt/moan and the pleasant voice inquired, "Esta bien, Pepe?" Pepe grunted in the affirmative.

I had noticed a light coming from under their door the whole time I was listening to all of this. It had started around 1:30. Now it was close to 4:00 a.m. The light went out. I had turned my TV off early on in this incident. Now I waited a little longer and, not hearing any sound whatsoever, I made my way into the bathroom and turned on that light which wouldn't be visible to anyone in the adjoining room. Quietly I got out the clothes I would wear the next day. I took a sponge bath and put on my clothes. I packed all the rest of my belongings and set my suitcase by the door. Then I sat, dressed and ready to bolt out the door if necessary. I was unable to go to sleep. I was scared out of my wits.

I sat there like that for three hours. Finally, although it wasn't yet 8:00 a.m., I opened the door quietly and slipped across the hall to see if Maria or Juan might be awake. I knocked very softly on their door. Maria opened it and cried, "Ah, Christina!"

I motioned for her to shush. I brushed past her and closed the door. I apologized for coming over so early and then I proceeded to tell her why. Her eyes widened as I told my story. Soon, Juan came out from the bathroom, fully dressed, and Maria told him what had happened. He looked at me and saw that I was terrified. He asked where my luggage was. I told him inside my door. He went to get it and brought it back to set beside their already packed bags.

Soon it was time to go down the hall and meet with the rest of our party, Juan was telling the story to Ricardo as we walked to the elevator. Ricardo looked skeptical, probably thinking that I was a hysterical female. But Juan and Maria knew me well enough to know I wasn't imagining things.

The hotel was a strange shape: a square shape with inner

corridors. The men went to stand at the desk, waiting for our luggage to be brought down. We three women and little Rosa went to a sunken living room-type of sitting room to wait for our luggage cart. My line of vision was in a straight line to the front entrance.

Maria was telling Ricardo's wide-eyed wife about what had happened. The front door opened and a huge, burly man walked in. He looked directly at me, sitting about 20 feet away. He had such a fierce look of hatred at the sight of me, I knew immediately he was one of the three. Then he continued on, past the registration desk, and on to the elevators.

I went over to Maria and Rosa and said, "That's one of them!" Their eyes widened.

Soon the man and two others came down the hall from the elevators. They did not glance in our direction but proceeded out the door of the hotel. Then Ricardo and Juan motioned for us to come on, our luggage cart was there.

We exited the hotel and started walking across the big parking lot to our SUV. As we were walking along, the three men who had left before we did came around us and the smaller of the three, nicely dressed, was speaking. It was the same voice with the same accent that I had listened to for hours in the early morning. They continued on and got into a little white truck that had lettering on the side. They drove off.

We loaded up our vehicle and headed over to another restaurant. It was a beautiful Saturday morning, sitting by the seaside in Vera Cruz. I was still very shaky. I asked Maria what the lettering was on their vehicle. She said that it indicated that it belonged to the government. She also said that thieves used vehicles like that as a cover.

After breakfast Juan said he wanted to go to a favorite store of his to get some shirts. All in all I figure we killed more than two hours before we started out on the treacherous highway that would take us to Guadalajara late the next afternoon. I was a nervous wreck on this ride. The highway itself was horrific enough with crazy drivers whizzing by, passing where it wasn't allowed, but in my frazzled, sleep-deprived condition it was terrifying. I was relieved when we stopped at a little out-of-the-way motel which had a rudimentary shower and I was able to bathe and lie down. My fear left me almost immediately and I was fine the next day, Sunday, as we continued on our going-home trip. Ricardo and the two Rosas would leave us at the Holiday Inn in Guadalajara. It was one of the most beautiful hotels I had ever seen. I had my own room with a balcony where I could sit and listen to the strolling musicians on the grounds below. I had absolutely no fear now just as I hadn't feared being by myself at any time on the whole trip, other than in the room in Vera Cruz and in the hotel lobby. Ricardo didn't believe that it was really a threat. Everybody else believed it.

About three weeks after I returned home my girlfriend Sylvia sent me a newspaper clipping from her local paper in Pennsylvania. It stated that a couple from Pittsburgh had been vacationing in Vera Cruz. Their bodies were found off the road, the same horrible road that we had been traveling on, the only main artery there is. They had been robbed, murdered, and their bodies left there. The article went on to say that authorities had tips that a white government vehicle was thought to have been involved.

My theory is that perhaps the thugs had been casing the hotel and its occupants, or maybe they were in cahoots with the hotel staff. Our group looked like rich, likely prospects: the "abuelo," grandfather, the "whetta", me with the camcorder, Juan and Maria, everybody well-dressed and Ricardo driving an expensive SUV. I thought back to the pleasant-sounding, mild one giving instructions in his hypnotic voice. One thing

SOMEONE IS WATCHING... AND WAITING.

I couldn't figure out at first was if he had given the others a shot of something, (because the light went out and I figured then that they had gone out to rob people). But how was it that they were still in the room when we were sitting in the lobby? How was the mean one able to come back into the hotel at 8:00 a.m.? Then I talked to a doctor friend. He told me there was a sleep-inducing drug that could be administered and it would seem like the person had had a much longer sleep.

Now I figured that they had staked us out to follow us and rob us. Maybe the first one had been sent out to eyeball the vehicles (re-enforcing the hotel staff theory) and was dumfounded and very angry when he came back into the hotel and saw me sitting there. He went on up to the room, informed his boss, they came down and pretended not to have any thoughts about us, but had the idea that they would follow us out of town. We upset the plans when we went to breakfast first and then went shopping in the downtown stores. Maybe they moved on to other quarry on the highway from Vera Cruz to Mexico City.

CHAPTER

12

NEW YEAR'S EVE SPANKER

I was working in real estate. I owned an office in town and it was reasonably successful. My name was listed under the business name as the owner, with my home number also, so it wasn't too unusual to get phone calls at home when I wasn't in the office. On this New Year's Eve day my telephone rang about 1:00 p.m.

"Hello, I'm Vincent and I just got into town. I'm interested in looking at some real estate here or in one of the neighboring towns."

I asked the usual questions: what kind of real estate, which areas are of the most interest, did you have a price range in mind, when did you want to begin looking?

"I realize you may have plans for tonight, being New Year's Eve and all?"

"Why yes, I do. Will you be in town for a few days?"

Then the caller proceeded to tell me about himself: he was coming from back East, he'd always heard about California, in fact had been here a few months before and had met me in a restaurant in San Diego."

I never forgot a face but I may not have remembered the name if I'd just had a quick introduction.

Vincent continued telling me about different businesses that he was involved with. And since he was looking for commercial property as well as a residence, I thought he might turn out to be a good prospect.

We talked about various things for 20-30 minutes and then Vincent said he had to touch base with a friend and that he would call me back in case my plans changed and we could go out for dinner.

He called about an hour later and this time he sounded friendlier, more familiar. In fact he started getting too familiar. He told me among his many business ventures was the manufacture of negligees. He asked me if I was married. I told him no. He asked me what color hair I had. This question tipped me off that he wasn't on the up and up.

"You said you met me once. Surely you would not forget that I have very red hair!"

He tried to side-step that by saying, "Yes, and you're beautiful! I can't imagine any man letting you go."

"It was MY choice!"

"Tell me, did your husband ever spank you?"

I bristled at these words, remembering the anonymous phone calls I got for many mornings in Pittsburgh, asking me the same question.

I became silent.

"What's the matter? Why aren't you talking?"

"Years ago a very strange man asked me that same question. I've got to go now."

"Okay, I'll call you later."

I didn't answer the phone when it rang a couple of times after that and the caller didn't leave a message.

Two weeks later I was at my desk in my office, reading the newspaper. There was an article at the bottom of the front page that requested that anyone having knowledge of mysterious phone calls to please contact a detective at the number that was provided. I dialed the number.

Detective Romero came into the office and my secretary directed him to my office. He introduced himself. I invited him to sit down and asked if he would like a cup of coffee. He declined.

"What can you tell me about the article you read in the paper?"

I began the story of Vincent's phone calls and our conversation.

"He's using a new alias and some of his stories have changed but some are the same. Did he try to set up a date with you?"

"Yes, but I already had plans. Then he called back to see if my plans had changed. That's when he made a couple of mistakes. I figured he wasn't for real. He was scary—somebody I didn't want to deal with."

"That was smart of you. This man has warrants out for his arrest in fives states: two in New England, Ohio, New Mexico and Arizona. When he hits a town he starts looking for possible victims: newly widowed women, which he's already discovered from scanning newspapers before he gets to the town, names in telephone books under just the woman's name—you were a prime target because of your name and the owner of a business as well. Then he makes his pitch.

"We figure this guy hit town about noon and started making his phone calls. He called you around one o'clock, probably thought you were going to be difficult so he would try some others. Didn't have much luck, so he called you back and got a little more aggressive. When he struck out he moved on to others. One of those was a widow in a neighboring town.

"They met. Apparently he wooed her and the next day they left town to go to Los Angeles. It was New Year's Day. They took the lady's Cadillac, her money and expensive jewelry that she thought she was going to wear at her wedding on January 2, when they were to drive to Las Vegas to get married. Then they would go on their honeymoon. They rented a nice hotel room in Los Angeles to wait for the wedding day.

"In the morning, the lady was alone. Really alone. Sometime in the night, the man, your "Vincent" had taken her car, her money and her jewelry and skipped town. We're still trying to run him down. Now he can add California to the states he's wanted in."

CHAPTER

13

HELP ME!

I was happy to be fixing up my new house and gardening, luxuries which I had not been able to indulge in, while I was married to my former husband and living in Wyoming. He was my second husband, a selfish, egotistical, and chauvinistic man. I was glad to be free of him and living on my own in this small getaway in Nevada.

There were many details for me to take care of now, but I was used to that. In my marriage I'd been the detail person. My ex-husband had left all that to me, happy to shrug off responsibility for everything that didn't involve fishing, hunting or sitting in the coffee shop with his cronies, shaking dice and telling tall tales.

I had hoped this move would turn out to be a good one and that here I could create a peaceful existence. I hoped that it would enable me to get involved with projects which were interesting to me; perhaps to dabble in writing or gardening, whenever and for as long as I wanted. Before, there had always been the thought lingering in the back of my mind that there would be work to go to early Monday morning. With Sunday, if then, being my only day off from my job as broker in the real estate office, I had never had enough time to devote to the things that I liked to do. Now, since I had taken an early retirement and obtained my divorce, I could relax a little and pursue other interests. My friends told me I was too young to retire but I had worked long hours all my life, sometimes seven days a week. Now I was able to do this, at this time in my life. I was ready for it and I felt I deserved it.

I had been here for two weeks, during which time I had been getting the house ready for my permanent occupancy. With that finished I could now concentrate on my true love, the garden.

I surveyed the project I had started of trying to beautify the yards, which were considerable on this two-acre parcel. I had two side yards, a front yard, a back yard and a way-back yard which was beyond the outbuildings and inner fence. There was extensive fencing. The property had established trees and shrubs with a drip irrigation system, which the former owner had planted and installed and about five tons of gravel but that was all. I had bought some solar yard lights and was anxious to see how they would look in my garden, which I intended to plant soon.

The yard had been a big selling point for me when my husband and I had bought the little house as a vacation retreat four years before, in this small community on the outskirts of Las Vegas.

The area where I lived was about three miles from the main section of town. There were a lot of homes, wide-open spaces and tumbleweeds between me and where the city began. My house was at the end of a short street with a stop sign in front of it. The neighborhood was a mishmash of meager homes and nicer ranch-style homes.

Directly across from me was a woman who appeared to be in her late thirties who had teenagers that I had observed coming and going, always seeming to be in a hurry. Their house was always vacated after about seven in the morning and stayed empty until evening. It was on a corner, like mine. Next to that and to its right was a conglomerate of eyesores: a couple of old empty trailers, a fork lift, a flatbed trailer with old salvaged lumber on it and at least one small trailer that I thought might be habitable. It had a tiny television antenna on its roof. I had heard from a man working in the gas station, that this neighbor was a hermit, sort of, who had made the statement that the reason he had moved from California to this town was so he could do anything he wanted to without authorities telling him otherwise. Maybe that explained the unsightliness of his two acres, the piles of lumber and overall appearance of a junkyard. I thought that the year before, the owner must have rented some of his space out to snowbirds, because I had talked to one of them one day when I went across the street to my mailbox. The fifth-wheel trailer that he had indicated as being his was not there now. But it was still too early for any of the snowbirds to be arriving. They usually didn't show up until late in November. This high desert town was a haven for people coming from colder climates looking for mild winter temperatures and low humidity

Two acres over from the junkyard was a nice looking, respectable ranch-style home. It was a rosy beige in color and I had seen a homemade sign out at the road, telling me that free iris bulbs were available. That seemed to be a friendly gesture and I thought that I would stop in and introduce myself and get some free bulbs. But for one reason or another I never made it. And then one day, I noticed the sign was gone.

I had never seen any of my neighbors, save for a brief glimpse of the woman with teenagers and a grey-haired man who rode his bicycle past my house in the morning. He had waved to me when he saw me out in the yard.

This October morning was pleasantly cool and quiet, as I

dug the first hole with my trowel and placed the glass light in it, adding dirt and pushing on it with my foot to firm up the earth around it. Then, searching for a good spot for the next one, I was startled when I heard a deep male voice crying out from across the street.

It bellowed out, "Help me! Somebody help me!"

Where did that come from? Alarmed, I peered across the street and waited to see if I heard any more. There was nothing. Oh, maybe somebody had their TV on or maybe he was having a bad dream, I thought. I eyed the row of yews and moved over to that area of the evergreens where I had decided to place the next light. I knelt down.

The silence was shattered when, again I heard, louder this time, "Help me! Somebody, help me!"

Okay, I thought. That does it. What are the chances of somebody having a bad dream twice and yelling out the same words? I straightened up and went to my front fence, thinking that somebody may have fallen and couldn't get up. Or maybe some of his junk had fallen on him and impaled him. I couldn't see any signs of life across the street. No movement of any kind.

I shouted, "Is somebody in trouble over there? "Do you need help? Where are you?"

I waited. Only silence. Should I call 911? What if it was only somebody having a bad dream? Besides, the guy could be dead by the time help got out to this remote area. But what could I do to help, with my shoulder not quite healed yet from the surgery I'd had six months before? I certainly couldn't lift anything very heavy. Maybe I should try to go to the other neighbor's house. What if they weren't home? Why hadn't they heard the voice? They were as close to it as I was. Maybe they were inside and couldn't hear it. I would be embarrassed if it turned out to be nothing at all. A dozen thoughts flitted through my brain.

Then I heard it again; the same loud cry for help. Maybe he hadn't heard me yell. I couldn't wait. I had to do something. Going into my house, I grabbed my cell phone and turned it on.

Something stopped me from running over to see what the trouble was. Instead, I took the key ring which held the car keys and the ones for the house, down from its peg inside the front door. It also held the key to the Ace lock on my front gate. I locked the front door behind me and ran to the fence and hurriedly opened the lock and swung the gates open. Hitting the keyless opener on the car keys, I piled into the maroon Infiniti SUV. I thought it more prudent to drive down the little lane by the mailboxes, which was the only access I could see. I locked the car door and lowered the window slightly on the driver's side.

I drove in about twenty feet and called out, "Is somebody in trouble here? HELLO! Do you need help?" I waited and heard nothing. Not a sound. I drove about twenty feet more and was abreast of the only structure which looked like it was habitable, the one with the TV antenna on it. I peered around the scattered debris all the while, in case someone was lying under it, but I saw nothing.

"Hello? Is anybody there? Are you hurt?"

The place was as still as death. I was certain from the volume and direction of the cries that they would have to have emanated from this area. I was also certain that if someone were in the tiny trailer and if he were alive, that my voice could be heard. Still I heard nothing.

Thinking that it was remotely possible that my ears had played tricks on me, as to the direction the cries had come from—although I had a very keen sense of hearing—I drove on down the dirt road, which I could see now that I was closer to it, led to a very respectable-looking, two-storied brick house.

SOMEONE IS WATCHING... AND WAITING.

It sat on the back of the property, well away from the junky mess up front. But then I saw that it had a six-foot cyclone fence around it and a sign hung on the gate, which read, "No Trespassing." I looked beyond the fence and couldn't see any signs of vehicles or people, so I backed up to a wider spot, where I could turn around. I now realized that this was too far away from where I'd been working in my yard for me to have heard the voice so clearly, if at all.

When I was abreast of the spot where I was sure the voice had come from, I called out again. No response. I continued driving and made up my mind that I would go to the house next door, The 'house of the Iris bulbs', as I had come to think of it.

As I pulled out onto the pavement, I saw the grey-haired bicycle rider coming down the street toward me. I continued forward slowly until he was even with my car. He held up his hand in a wave.

I called out to him, "Can you help me, please?"

The grey-haired man stopped his bike. "What's the trouble?" He looked concerned as he got off and wheeled his bike over to my driver's door.

"I think someone in that trailer over there," and I indicated the one that I meant, "is in trouble. He was calling out for help!"

"That one there?"

"Yes! I called to him but he didn't answer."

"Okay, I'll go see what's up." He wheeled his bike into the yard and laid it down at the steps of the small brown and white trailer, calling out as he did so.

"Somebody hurt in there?" He banged on the side of the trailer.

Silence.

He hurried up the steps and pounded on the door. "Hey! You in there! Are you hurt? Do you need help?"

Silence.

"Guess I'll have to try to get in," the neighbor shouted.

Just then I could hear a faint muffled voice inside the trailer saying something.

"What's the matter? Are you all right?"

The man listened and then called to me, "He says he was just calling his dog."

I had remained in my car, with the window halfway down while this was happening.

"'Calling his dog'! What's his dog's name?" I didn't believe this!

Just then a quieter voice but with the same timbre that I'd heard before, called from inside the trailer, "Here, Brownie."

After the helpful neighbor had wheeled his bike back into the street, he introduced himself as Bob Miller. His wife, who had been walking along briskly, caught up to us. She came over to the driver's window and offered her hand. "My name's Carol. Welcome to the neighborhood. Come up and see us sometime. We live in the big white ranch house at the beginning of the street."

"Thank you. I'll do that." I smiled at her. And I promised myself that I would.

I decided, since I was in my Infiniti already, that I would go on into town. I pondered what had just happened as I drove down the back streets to the hardware store. Had my lively imagination played tricks on me? Had I really heard the cries? Yes!, I thought emphatically. I had heard it distinctly, all three times, "Help me, somebody help me!" And that didn't sound anything like, "Here Brownie!" But why would the guy lie to the neighbor? Could he have been dreaming? Once, maybe even allowing for twice which was a stretch, but it was impossible to believe that it could have happened exactly like that three times. Simple logic told me that that was not a reasonable explanation.

I thought I would check out the hardware store, to see what sort of security devices they sold. I didn't have a gun, nor did I want one. All I had at the present time was a hammer that I took to bed with me and the phone. But I realized that a phone call to the police for help could take five or ten minutes for them to get there, best-case scenario. That was enough time for somebody to do what they wanted and get out of my house and run away. I also had dusk-to-dawn security lights in the front and on the side but there was an area in the back that was unprotected, completely dark.

I decided the next time I was out and about that I would stop at the neighbor's house, and give Carol my telephone number and get hers in return, so that help could be just up the street, if I needed to make a phone call. Also, I would go to the garage, pull one of my golf clubs out of the bag and keep it in the house with me.

Every time I thought about the incident of the morning, I became angry. What kind of game was that man playing?

That night I installed the battery operated devices which would emit a high-pitched screech if an intruder opened the door while the button was set. I took a hammer, the aluminum baseball bat that I had decided to buy and the cordless phone and went to bed.

Two days later, as I was driving home from the Post Office I decided to take Carol up on her offer of, "Stop and see us sometime." I had never been one to thrust myself on other people, even though I didn't mind much when other people were aggressive about getting to know me and tried to become my friend. I had been reticent about forming new relationships, but the few times that I had impulsively introduced myself to others had turned out well. I had made two lifelong friends that way. Most people are usually gregarious by nature, I told myself, encouragingly, and Carol did say to stop and see them. Besides I didn't want these new neighbors to get the impression that I was an oddball who imagined voices. I thought that something further needed to be said about the incident. And I was still curious.

I pulled into the graveled driveway of the large white ranch-style house. It had Halloween decorations on the porch. Well, that's nice and friendly, I thought as I got out of my SUV.

Carol's husband Bob had emerged from the huge storage building over at the side of their property and was coming toward me, smiling as he called out, "Well, hello there!"

"Hi," I called back. "I hope I'm not coming here at an awkward time." The fact is I had considered it and thought 11:00 a.m. would be a good time, breakfast would be over and done with and it was too early for lunch.

"Oh, certainly not! C'mon, we'll go inside. I'm ready to take a break anyway."

He opened the door for me, which led into a quietly tasteful, family room. "Carol's probably back in the computer room. Honey!" he called out, "we have company."

Carol emerged, looking a little distracted.

"Oh, I don't want to intrude on what you were doing," I protested.

"Not at all," Carol graciously told me. "Sit down. Can I offer you something to drink?"

"Oh, no, that's kind of you, but no thank you. I just wanted to stop and say hi but I did have a question for you. Do you happen to have a doctor that you could recommend? Since I'm going to be spending a lot of time here I should get established with some medical people."

Carol busied herself with getting the telephone book and

finding the number of a doctor she had gone to. "Here it is. For dentists and specialists, I usually go into the city but in an emergency, this is a good doctor to call." She wrote a number on a piece of paper and handed it to me.

I admired the home and its décor. Carol told me various things about the home and Bob contributed by adding tidbits about the construction, grading, and utilities, which I told him would be useful to me in the future, if I decided to put a new home on the acre, which adjoined the property where I lived now. I owned it too and had given serious thought to doing this.

I had been trying to guess what their reaction would be when I brought up the subject of my neighbor again. I had waited until I thought we were all feeling relaxed enough in our conversation.

Finally I began, "I'd like to say something about what happened the other day. I don't want you to think I'm some kind of a kook, or an alarmist, but I've thought and thought about it and I just don't believe that guy was calling his dog."

Bob looked at me for a moment and then said pleasantly enough, "Well, maybe he was just having a bad dream."

I asked, "Do you know anything about him? What sort of person is he?"

"I had him, well actually I think it was his brother, do some grading work for me when we first came here. He's a little strange, got some weird ideas, but I think he's probably all right. He did say that the reason he moved here was to get out of California and to be able to do whatever he wanted to do, without a bunch of rules."

That was the second time I had heard that he had made that statement.

"You don't think he's dangerous? Or deranged?"

"No, I wouldn't think so."

"Well, why didn't he answer me, when I called out to him?"

"Maybe he didn't hear you.

I think he did, I thought, but I didn't want to push it. "Well, if he was having a bad dream, why didn't he just say so, instead of telling you he was calling his dog?"

"I really think the guy was having a bad dream. He was zipping up his pants as he came to the door, like he'd been sleeping."

I tried not to show any concern over that statement and what it might imply.

"What does he look like?"

"He has a long, grayish-white beard."

"A Santa Clause type, huh?" I smiled weakly.

"No, he's pretty thin."

I decided to change the subject. "You know, Carol, I don't know anyone here, except for friends who live 10 miles across town. I wonder if I could take your telephone number in case I ever have an emergency."

"Oh, you surely can. Bob, where are those business cards we used to give out? They have our e-mail address on them too."

"That's a good idea. Here, I'll write mine down for you, too."

I said goodbye and invited them to stop to see me, "Anytime. Stop in anytime."

I decided to bounce the incident off my daughter to see what her thoughts were on it. That night when I was sure Theresa would be home from work, I dialed her number. My daughter worked as a microbiologist in California and had a clinical, logical mind.

After the usual catching up on news, I said, "Tree, I'd like to ask your opinion on something."

"Yes, Mom?"

I told my daughter all of the details, giving the proper inflection and emphasis to the cries for help.

"So, what do you think?"

"I think he sounds like a nut! Mom, I don't like you living there by yourself!"

Hearing the concern in my daughter's voice, I said, "I keep all the doors locked, and the gates. He'd have to work pretty hard to get in. Then, if he did, I'd have my hammer to clobber him with. And now, I have an aluminum baseball bat." I laughed. "Besides, I asked a neighbor what he thought and he said he doesn't think he's dangerous."

"Yeah, well, nobody thought Ted Bundy was dangerous either."

"Well, I think by bringing the neighbor into it, the guy now knows that I'm not alone in thinking he was up to something, innocent or not."

"He was probably sitting at his window, watching you working in your garden. Then, just like kidnappers do, he tried to enlist your help, tried to get you to go to his territory. It's a good thing you didn't go walking over there alone!"

"No, I would never do that. But I didn't feel I could just do nothing at all. He sounded desperate."

"Promise me that if you have the slightest feeling that you're in trouble that you will call that neighbor. Immediately!"

"Yes," I said. "I've already put their number on my speed dial."

My friend, Monica called the next day. After catching each other up on the latest news from the town I had just moved out of, in Wyoming, I said, "I want to tell you something that happened here. I told my story, finishing up with, "So, what do you think?"

Monica answered grimly, "I'd hate to tell you what I think."

A week later I stopped in my favorite casino that was close to the post office, where I kept a box, to pick up the morning's mail. I liked to play the penny poker machines. I told myself that a couple of dollars for an hour or so of amusement never hurt anything. And sometimes I actually won a few dollars. Apparently this was one of those times, for I noticed that my points had totaled up to twelve dollars. I'd been playing for about half an hour, at a bank of four penny machines. The place was practically empty. Nobody else was playing where I sat down. I ordered a diet Coke from the waitress who worked the floor. I didn't pay any attention when someone sat down at the end seat, two over from mine. My machine hit again for four of a kind. This was fun!

The waitress brought my Coke, set it down and turned to ask the newcomer if he wanted something.

"Yeah, rum and Coke." It was the same voice that had cried out three times for help a week ago!

I didn't want to look at him. I didn't want him to know that I recognized his voice. I pushed the button for the machine attendant to cash out. I tried to remain calm as I sipped on the diet Coke and surreptitiously glanced sideways. His eyes were fixed on the machine in front of him. His lean gaunt face wore a long, thin, greyish-white beard. He didn't seem to be paying any attention to me.

The attendant brought my money and I eased out of my chair. I tried to remain calm and act as if nothing were amiss. I did not want the man to realize that I knew who he was, I hurriedly left the casino. I was afraid, but at the same time I felt cowardly to feel like that. Wasn't this person infringing on my rights? Who did he think he was?

Nevertheless, every time I drove into town after that, I nervously looked in my rear-view mirror to see if the little, grey Pinto was behind me.

SOMEONE IS WATCHING... AND WAITING.

A week later I stopped in the market. As I was leaving I decided to take a route back to my house that I didn't normally take. I always liked to explore different roads and streets and see new things. Two blocks down this road I glanced in the rear view mirror. The little grey Pinto was about eight car lengths behind me! I sped up and made a couple of turns and got back on the shortest way to my house. When I pulled up at my gates I noticed that the grey Pinto wasn't in it's usual parking spot.

One month later, I was raking leaves and grass on an extremely warm afternoon. I was wearing a red, terrycloth one-piece shorts outfit with a strapless halter top. I hated to lose the tan I had worked on over the summer, so I took advantage of every chance I got to soak up some sun.

I waved at the mail delivery woman in her little blue mail car, as she deposited mail in the boxes, which stood in a line across the street from my yard.

Soon, I saw the white SUV, belonging to the neighbor, who lived down the lane and on the far side of the strange neighbor's property, drive slowly up the lane, toward the mailboxes. He must have come down early this year, I thought. I glanced up and saw him retrieve the mail from his box. Then he backed his vehicle around so that the driver's side was closest to me. He waved and grinned at me. I smiled and waved back. I went back to pulling stubborn weeds out of a particularly difficult spot. I had turned away from the street to do this and when I straightened up and looked back, I saw the white SUV still sitting there with the man inside it watching me.

I thought that maybe he wanted to say something. I smiled hesitantly as I looked at the driver and brushed a blonde curl off my face. He said nothing and slowly drove away. Is this town full of weirdoes? I wondered to myself, or am I becoming paranoid?

The next day I spent inside the house, working on my computer, and attending to a long list of household chores that my gardening had caused me to neglect.

But the following day I was out in the yard at 8:00 a.m. I had some trees that needed pruning and I wanted to do it early, before the unseasonably warm afternoon set in. I was getting my pruning shears out of the potting shed when I heard the voice of the weird neighbor from across the street call out. Glancing up I saw him standing in his front yard. That's interesting, I thought cynically, I could have sworn that he sleeps in much later, considering those 'dreams' that made him call out, "Help me!" a month before.

The man made a pretense of not paying any attention to me and only calling innocently to his dog. This was the first time I had seen the animal, but sure enough, there sniffing the ground for an appealing spot on which to relieve itself, was what appeared to be a beagle or terrier.

Without showing any surprise, I continued to collect my gardening tools. But when I bent down to pick up a gardening glove that I had dropped, my eyes traveled up and I saw that the man was intently watching me. He quickly turned away as I stood up.

"C'mon, Boo-Boo," he growled at the little brown and white dog, as he turned to walk away. Apparently his Brownie had become a Boo-Boo.

Soon after this my friend Monica moved into my house and she worked in Las Vegas. She brought Rio, her German Shepherd with her. Rio stayed with me in the daytime while Monica worked. Rio barked at strangers. Monica had a gun. I had no more fears while living in that house. And I never heard from the neighbor across the street again.

14

THE PEACOCK PURSUER

I was standing in my kitchen one morning, in rural California, waiting for my coffee to brew and looking out the kitchen window. I could see something waving at me from the bank outside my chain link fence. What is that? I wondered. I decided to go take a look.

There, stuck way down in the bare dirt, was a beautiful peacock feather, its plume wafting in the light, gentle breeze. It had been placed there for me in my direct line of sight from the kitchen window, and since no one else had any occasion to go into this area, I assumed it was for my sole benefit. But why? And by whom? And when?

I went outside. I tried to replicate its getting there by any means other than human effort. I repeatedly tried to drive it into the earth by sending it there with force. It failed every time. I wondered if there was any other possible way that the bird could have lost his plume and then it being picked up by a hurricane-force wind and being driven into the ground. But we hadn't had any such winds. And this was a highly unlikely, if not impossible scenario. It took a great deal of twisting, screwing, and forcing the quill down into the earth and then packing up dirt around it to get it to stand erect. I had to conclude that my quirky neighbor, who happened to be the only one in town who raised peacocks, had planted it there. As a gift for me perhaps? Or as a prank to see what my reaction would be, for it was in a direct line with the rear windows of his house, about 1000 feet away, and in plain sight, especially if you had binoculars.

I need to add one reinforcing note here: This same neighbor had a reputation for being quirky. His property was the only one adjacent to mine. One morning when I was getting ready to go to the airport, I stepped off my patio to feed the birds in my backyard. I approached the fence which divided his land from mine.

In the stillness of the early morning a voice bellowed out, "Hey Blondie!"

Startled, I looked up to see who it was or where it had come from. I could see nothing save for a large amount of trees and brush. I assumed the owner of the bellowing voice had hidden behind something and was too shy to show himself. Or too devious. Later I found the peacock feather and later still, a full can of Miller's Highlife beer, opened, which had been planted in the dirt on this apron surrounding my property. Later there were more empty beer cans and a cigarette lighter.

This is the house where I live now.

CHAPTER

15

DON, THE MOST-WANTED CON

Valentine's Day. This was the day that I would meet one of the most mysterious persons that I have ever encountered. He didn't appear to be that, until he had gone out of my life. He seemed to be a poor, lost soul seeking something to replace a light, a beacon that had disappeared from his life. Looking back, after discovering facts about him much later, it's chilling to think that I shared time with a person who had been on America's Most Wanted list, that he had lain beside me and told me of his dreams.

I was sitting at music venue, in the California desert. It was on a Friday evening, Valentine's Day. I had gone up earlier in the afternoon, stopped at Sandi's art place and purchased three pieces of her folk art. Her trailer had been a favorite stop for me on my many trips to see a friend of mine at his artist's retreat.

I had been here in January, a month before, after talking on a dating site with one of the snowbird residents who winters at this desert getaway. We had agreed to meet on Wednesday for our first date at a local park and we talked while his friendly dog cavorted around. Lawrence seemed very intelligent, looked clean, drove a nice, new jeep and was very caring of his dog, who also looked clean and both of them looked well-groomed.

This attention to one's person was not always evident in some of the people, those who had no plumbing or electricity. Then we, Lawrence and I made a date for lunch at a Chinese restaurant on the following Saturday. After that we were to go to listen to the

I had hopes of finally having someone I could go with to The Ridge to hear some of the music which was reportedly very good. I had never been there because I hated to go anywhere alone and that was especially so in this strange environment which had no public utilities and from what I had seen on my previous visits in the daytime, had some rather questionable-looking characters hanging around. I'd asked various friends and family to go with me but no one was interested in going. I was curious to hear the music.

Lawrence and I had enjoyed the music immensely and I was determined to go back but then my trip was delayed because I went up to the Bay Area to spend three weeks with my daughter, so I couldn't return until Valentine's Day.

Stopping at Sandi's I asked her if she was going to go to the music thing and if she went was she going to sing. She told me she hadn't sung at the previous night of music as there were many artists who wanted to take to the stage and she had many more opportunities than most of them had, since she lived there full time. Sandi told me yes, tonight, she was going to sing. I told her I would go say hello to my friend, Lawrence, and I would come back before sundown, when the music was ready to begin and maybe we could go together.

I went to say hello to my friend and told him I was going back to pick Sandi up and go to listen to the music. He didn't want to go but he said I would need to take a chair because the seating was limited so he got one of his folding chairs and loaded it in the trunk of my car. I promised that I would return it to him.

"Hi, I'm Chef. And you are?"

I eyed the tall stranger who was dressed in a white chef's coat and slouch hat. His voice was very mellow.

"I'm Christina. Is Chef really your name?"

"Well, no, that's just what they call me." He held out his hand, "Don, Chef Don. Would you like a Margarita?" He indicated the pitcher he was holding which appeared to be filled with a pale liquid.

"Oh, no thanks, I bring my own." I held up my to-go cup of vodka and diet Coke.

I observed him as he scurried around filling up people's cups. One of the other men came over and handed me a Valentine's card, and a little box of candy hearts, saying, "May I give this to you and wish you a happy Valentine's day?"

I thought that this was a very friendly place.

Don sat down a few chairs over from where Sandi had told me to put my chair, saying mine was the best spot. There was nobody sitting between us and we chatted a little- just small talk. He told me about the Valentine's dinner he had just cooked of prime rib, twice-baked potatoes, asparagus au gratin, and Cherries-Jubilee. Then the place started to fill up and a lady sat in the chair between Don and me and started talking to Don, saying that she wanted to ask him some things about Italy, as she was planning a trip there. I continued listening to the music. At a break, when I could hear myself speak, I said to her that I had overheard her mention of Italy and since I had been there I was anxious to talk about it. We had a lengthy conversation, with Don and the two women sitting on his left contributing bits here and there. He had introduced everybody to me as they appeared. Then when some of these women left, Don moved over to the seat beside me. He invited me to come on Sunday morning to the brunch that he was going to cook for the people. It was going to be at The Oasis at 11:00 a.m. He explained where that was.

Sunday morning found me at the Desert Hideaway a little before 11:00 a.m. Some hippie-looking kids were walking out of what I thought was The Oasis. I rolled down my window and asked if this was where the brunch was being held.

"Yes, but it's over."

Over?

I parked my car and walked up to what looked like had once been a food line. Don was standing there with three women. He recognized me and said, "Here she is!"

I said, "I could have been here sooner but you said eleven."

"I know. They changed the time to nine. I was going to go find Sandi and ask her if she knew how to get a hold of you so I could tell you. And I was hoping you'd come to the music last night at The Range. I even brought a bottle of vodka because you said that's what you drink. I don't know what you mix with it but I had several things go with it."

I thought that was very observant of him and thoughtful to remember what I'd said about drinking vodka.

One of the ladies said something to him and Don said to me, "These gals are going to the Fountain of Youth Spa. They're having a 'Testicle Festival.' They told me I can go too but I don't want anything to do with that. Besides I've got to cook breakfast for this lady. I promised her." He motioned to me.

The ladies urged me to go with them and Don said, sure I should go, but I really didn't want to. I told him I could go for a cup of coffee though and he said for me to come with him over to another food venue where there was a big urn of coffee. I drove over with Don walking alongside my car, directing me.

I sat down on a bench as Don poured me a cup. I told him I hoped it wasn't too strong. Ordinarily I drink decaf but I thought I could handle a little caffeine. He said no, it was pretty tame. We moved over to a long table which was normally used to serve meals to the citizens of the Desert Hideaway. A couple of people wandered over and Don was polite and friendly to them.

Don told me about himself. His wife of 42 years had died about eight years before. He had loved her passionately and was devastated by her death. He didn't care if he lived or died. He had wandered around since, going from campground to RV park, and on to still another campground. Tears welled up in my eyes as I imagined this poor wretched man, bereft of his wife, who it seemed had also been his reason living, his existence.

Don told me about his two sons: that one, Michael, was a plastic surgeon. "We call him a boob doctor."

"Oh, I could probably use him," I said, laughing.

"No, you look fine to me," Don said shyly.

Michael's wife, Don's daughter-in law, Tammy had nursed him back to health, spoon-fed him in fact, when his wife died. She now ran all the business affairs, of which there seemed to be many.

Don said his other son, Kevin, was in the scrap metal business and told me how lucrative it was and that he made more money than the doctor did. Don then told me that he'd had a heart attack and a stroke, but "Nothing for a year and a half now."

I asked him how they had treated his heart attack and he said they put stents in. He said his son had done it and I questioned him on this, because a plastic surgeon would not have put stents in. He amended this to say he meant that his son had observed the surgery. I told him that I too had had open heart surgery, five years ago. He asked how my health was and I told him I'd had no problems. He said that he was supposed to take all sorts of medicine but he didn't take any of it.

I told him where I lived in and had for the past seven years, when I bought the house that came up for sale which was next door to my youngest daughter's house. Before that I had been living in a community on the outskirts of Las Vegas. He said that he had friends there too, who had gone there with an RV and liked it so well they bought a place in a park there. I told him that I had lived here in the valley before and I got married and moved to Wyoming where I lived for 12 years until I divorced my second husband and moved to Las Vegas. I had worked in real estate in all those places but retired when I moved to Nevada.

"I would have guessed that you were in real estate, you just seem to have that quality about you."

I asked him what he had done before, what kind of work he had done. He said that he'd been a corporate chef for a large hotel chain, going from place to place with his wife, to instruct chefs and do what corporate chefs did. He said his wife wrote music. I asked him where his chef's duties took him and he mentioned a few places. I remembered from Friday night that he had talked to the lady about Italy so I asked him where he had been in Italy.

"All over the place."

I wanted to know if he'd visited Venice and if so, if he'd seen the Doge's Palace. He told me that on these trips he didn't have much of a chance to go sightseeing but that his wife had. He said his wife's name was Valerie. I told him that was a coincidence because when I was thirteen, I had told people I wanted them to call me Valerie. And another coincidence was that I was working on a book entitled Donny and Me. I asked him where he had been in this part of California, that there were a lot of sights to see. He said he knew it from the outside but had never gone inside it.

"When can we go?" Don wanted to know.

I was always anxious to show people places I had seen. "We can go anytime. How about tomorrow?"

After thinking for a minute he said no, that he had a bunch of stuff he had to do on Monday. How about Tuesday? I told him that would work. I asked him if he had seen the metal art by Palm Springs and he said no, he hadn't. I told him we would have to do that on a day trip sometime. He seemed to be really enthused about seeing these various places with me. And that suited me fine. I loved to show people places I had discovered.

I noticed that he had a cut on his neck. "What's that from?"

He brushed at it, "What?"

"It looks like you nicked yourself."

"Yeah, probably when I shaved this morning. This isn't the best place to do that. Hey, you know what? You are so easy to talk to. I can't get over it, that I found somebody like you, here at this place

Then he asked me if I'd seen the Artist's Grotto. I told him I'd read about it but I hadn't seen it yet. He said we would go there. "It's here in the Hideaway."

We had been talking for about two hours when a Jeep drove up with a man and woman, who got out to come over to talk to Don. The man said he wanted to discuss having Don cook a Chinese dinner for his group. Don told him we were just about to go to The Artist's Grotto. so he could show it to me. Had they ever been there? They should see it. It was really something. He told the man that we would come back to his place in an hour or so and they would talk about the dinner.

We went to The Artist's Grotto on the other side of the

Desert Hideaway from where Don's trailer was. I like folk art, art made out all sorts of things. And the ingenuity of these artists who can create art from bottles, bottle caps, car parts etc. impressed me. And this place was full of extraordinary art. Then Don told me that the owner had invited us to come into the back, where outsiders didn't frequent, where only his "tribe" went. I said I guessed I was dressed appropriately enough because I had worn my Thunderbird T-shirt. We went into a cave-like room which had a bar upon which sat a pitcher of Margaritas. Don asked me if I wanted one and I accepted the red plastic cup, rimmed with salt. We sipped on our drinks as we talked to others in this friendly place, among them Stickman. We walked outside and I noticed that Don had a few flecks of salt at the corner of his mouth. I brushed it away and he said, "I can think of a better way to do that." I lightly kissed the remaining salt flecks away.

Don said, "You know what that means, don't you?"

"No, what?"

"That means we have to get married now." We laughed.

Don showed me various rooms in the place and jokingly said that I could probably rent one of them if I wanted to stay up there. I told him no, thanks, I liked a bed to sleep in.

Then he said, "Come over here!"

In this room there was a rather dilapidated bed. He joked that he was going to put a sign outside that this was Christina's Room.

After learning some of the history of the place, we left and Don asked me if I'd seen the Internet Café. I told him no. He said, "Well, let's swing over by it, but it's a joke, so don't expect too much."

He told me how to get there, which took us right by my friend Lawrence's place. He said, "We call this Snob Hill. He was referring to the many large motor homes, some of which, like Lawrence's, had solar panels and receiver-like equipment, which afforded them some of the basics to which they had become accustomed to in civilization. Don pointed to a spot on a little hill across and down the road from Lawrence's.

"That's where I'm going to set up my motor home when my sons bring it over next week." I asked him what kind it was. "A forty foot Monaco", which I assumed was a top of the line, and found out later that it was.

We stopped at the Internet café, which lived up to Don's description of not being much. It had various characters hanging around. Some of them looked pretty substantial, others did not.

One of the men came over to us and Don said hello to him and introduced us. "This is Christina and we've decided that we're going to get married and we think we may want to do it here."

The man laughed and said, "Sure!" Then Don jokingly began describing our supposed impending nuptials.

Then Don directed me on how to find his trailer. He told me that he had just bought it not long ago. He said, "If you are ever up here and need to use the restroom just come here. You're welcome to do that, even if I'm not home."

I said that was a good idea because when I drink I like to know where a bathroom is and not have to go searching for one. He said if I didn't want to drive home to just come here. He pointed to a small blue tent that was set up on a large indoor-outdoor carpet square in front of his trailer. I laughed and told him that I didn't relish the thought of a stray dog fighting me for space. He said, "Or you could go into the trailer. There's a bedroom in the back and nobody will bother you."

The couple drove up. Don said he would call me in an hour after he had finished with his plans for the Chinese dinner. I gave him my house phone number. I told him thanks for the nice time and the coffee. I left for home.

I stopped at a cafe on the way home and bought a couple of chicken wings. I hadn't had anything to eat all day and it was now after three o'clock. When I got home there was a message on my machine.

"This is Don. Looks like I missed you. Well, I'll call you in a little bit."

Sure enough the phone rang about 10 minutes later. We talked for a while, with Don telling me again, that he couldn't believe that he had met somebody like me. He couldn't believe that he could be that lucky. He told me that his cell phone needed to be charged and that he was using his friend's (Clarence's) phone. Don said he told him, "My phone's dead and I have to use yours. This is the most important phone call of my life!"

He told me he was going to play poker later but he hoped to take a nap first because he had been up late the night before and up quite early that morning. He said he always got up very early.

I asked him if he was any good at poker. He said, "Yeah, I'm good. I'm very good! In fact, I'm a professional poker player. I like to go to Vegas and play.

"Where do you play in Vegas?"

"Mostly at Binion's."

"Well, if you're that good, I probably won't want to play with you." I laughed.

After I hung up, I called my friend Jane in Carlsbad. She knew that I had a breakfast date with a fellow I'd met on Friday night. I talked to her telling her that this was a really nice guy and I told her some of the stuff he'd been telling me. I said that he was either the most adroit liar I'd ever met or he was on the up and up. Either way he was very knowledgeable about a wide variety of subjects. I mentioned that he had played poker in Las Vegas, at Binion's.

"Really? Next time you talk to him ask him if he knows . . ." and she named two men.

These are guys I knew at Binion's when I worked in Vegas. If this guy is for real he has to know these two men."

We hung up and soon I took a look at my calendar and saw that I had a doctor's appointment on Tuesday so the trip to Riverside wouldn't work. I went in to check the number that Don had called me from on my house phone. But I had to use my cell phone to call him back, because I don't use the house phone for long distance and Clarence's number was out of state, from Oregon. Clarence answered and I told him who I was and could I speak to Don.

Clarence said, "I think I see Don coming now. Hey Don! It's Christina."

Don got on and said, "I heard the phone ring and I was hoping it was you."

Again he went on and on about how lucky he was to have found me. Suddenly life had new meaning for him. He was touchingly romantic. I told him why I was calling, that we would have to change our plans. Then we decided that I would pick him up at his trailer on Tuesday morning at 9:00 a.m. I said that I'd talked to my friend, Jane and she used to work in Vegas and she told me to ask him if he knew the names she had mentioned.

He paused, as if he was recalling and said, "Yes, I know . . . . and he knows me."

"And . . . .?"

"No, I don't think I know him."

A later conversation with Jane ensued with her wanting names and places so she could check up on Don. Jane used to work for a detective agency and she was curious about everybody and especially this strange person I had just met.

I didn't talk to Don at all on Monday. He had told me he was going to be very busy. He said if he could find somebody to bring him into town it would save me from having to pick him up at the Desert Hideaway but I didn't get a phone call to change our plans. We had decided we would need to postpone the trip to Riverside.

Tuesday morning I showered and dressed rather sedately but I thought appropriate for my doctor's visit in the afternoon. I thought Don and I would have breakfast at 9-9:30, spend quite a bit of time talking and then maybe do something after my appointment, possibly go back to my town and listen to karaoke at the RV place at Sunshine Lake, or go back up to the Desert Hideaway to listen to their Tuesday night music. I didn't know what the day would entail but I was open to suggestions.

We had agreed to meet at 9:00 a.m. at John's trailer. Then we would go into town for breakfast. I had asked him about the restaurant in the next town, which I had stopped at to get ice on Friday with a diet coke. I had also wanted to use their restroom, which was not a plentiful commodity at the Desert Hideaway. So it was sort of Use One When You See One! Don told me the restaurant was okay.

I set out for the 45 minute drive to the Desert Hideaway at a little after 8:00 a.m. I like to be punctual for everything if not a little early, a habit from my days in real estate that I had not discarded when I retired. It always made me feel that I was in control as I observed other people as they arrived and what their mannerisms and reactions were. I thought I might be a few minutes late by the time I reached Don's trailer as I'd had to be careful of some early morning walkers on the road before I reached my destination.

SOMEONE IS WATCHING... AND WAITING.

I passed the sign that announces the Desert Hideaway and saw a man standing in the wide. barren stretch of sand. He waved. I waved back, thinking that he looked pretty spiffy for this early in the morning and especially in this place. Then he waved frantically. I had gone past him about 200 feet when I slowed down. Was that Don? He was the right height. I turned around, rather than making a right turn which would have taken me to Don's trailer. Slowly, I pulled up alongside the man who wore no slouch hat like Don had worn. He was dressed in white pants and a black, silky-looking short-sleeved shirt, much as you would expect to find in one of the beach cities. He was completely transformed from the Don Peterson I had met, now looking more like a wealthy playboy, rather than a poor, wandering ex-corporate chef, who seemed to have discarded his former life

"I didn't recognize you!" I cried, as I pulled up alongside him.

"I knew you didn't. I could tell. I just thought I'd meet you down here."

He climbed in the car. "Listen, can I ask you to do something before we go to breakfast?"

"What is it?"

"Can we stop at the Internet Café? I've got to pick up something there."

I wasn't beyond thinking that Don might be involved in drugs, especially now that I saw him dressed so well in his fine clothes. Well, I would keep my eyes and ears open for any sign of that.

"Sure, I guess so."

"Let's head over there and I'll explain on the way."

"Here's what happened," Don began his saga, "I'm always getting myself into these situations but I can't help it. I promised to help this girl whose boyfriend was beating up on her. She didn't have anybody to help her and she was trying to get away from him. I told her I would take her stuff from the Café to someplace where she could pick it up later."

"Where is that?"

"I'm not sure yet. She's supposed to call me when she knows."

We pulled up at the Café and Don hopped out to go find somebody. As it turned out it was the guy I'd met on Sunday, who ran the place. They came walking out of the back of the tent-like place with a couple of big backpacks and two rolled up things that looked like they might have been chairs like the one I had in my storage shed. They fold up and fit down a big sleeve-type sack. I got out of the car and said hello to the guy with Don and opened the trunk. I helped them fit the stuff in. It didn't look anything like drugs, although I'd never seen how they ship drugs. This looked like somebody's meager belongings, including one or two folding chairs. Don said goodbye and we left.

"Where are we going for breakfast?" I wanted to know. "What about that place you mentioned?"

"Would you mind if we found some other place? This one over here isn't so great. And that way I can explain about this girl."

"Okay, I know of a Mexican place. Is that okay? I'm sure they have American food too, if you don't want Mexican."

So, on the 18 mile ride to the restaurant, Don explained about the girl, Monica. She had gotten into a terrible fight with her boyfriend, who was drunk and hitting her. Don had intervened and told her he would help her. He asked her if she was sure she wanted his help? Yes, she wanted to move away from the guy and she would gather all her belongings and she wondered if Don could manage to get them out of the Desert Hideaway and to a place to store them until she could find somebody to help, then they would drive her to pick them up. She had stayed the night with these friends. It would probably be after five o'clock before the friends could take her to get her things, as they worked and also had kids in school in a nearby town. Monica had mentioned a Baptist church, that she knew the minister there.

"Do you know this girl?" I asked.

"Nope. Didn't know her from Adam."

"Why would you do this for someone you don't know?"

"I just couldn't stand to see her getting beat up like that. She was sobbing and asking for somebody to help her. Nobody else was making a move. I'm able to help and I just figured I would. Poor girl; her head is half shaved, she's got tattoos all over her. She said her family all disowned her. She's got nobody."

Tears had started to form in my eyes as I pictured her and I felt like I wanted to help this poor creature too.

"Do you think there's any chance of the boyfriend talking her into staying with him?"

"Well, if that happens then I'll wash my hands of her." He told me that he'd helped young people before to get back on the right path. He thought they deserved a chance but if this girl blew it then that was it.

While we were waiting for a booth to be cleaned in the restaurant, I told Don I needed to use the Ladies' room. He said, he'd take this opportunity to have a cigarette. This was the first I knew that Don smoked. He had not on Friday night when I met him and sat listening to music, nor had he in all the time I spent with him on Sunday. I had not noticed the odor of smoke on him but I hadn't spent that much time with him and very little of that was in an enclosed space. This might prove to be a problem in the future.

I said, "Oh, I didn't know you smoked."

He said, "Yeah, it's a bad habit, I know, but I could quit for you."

He ordered breakfast, asking the waitress if she could make him a hamburger patty with eggs, over easy.

Don said that he had tried to call the girl and didn't get her. He was going to find out where the Baptist place was but that it might be inconvenient to find. He also said that he was going to buy her a bus ticket to San Diego and that he had called his son and daughter-in-law and that they were going to get her a job in one of the restaurants they were involved with. I suggested that if that were the case, we would have enough time before I had to go to my doctor's appointment to drive into town and get the ticket. Then I could keep my appointment and possibly do something later that afternoon or evening.

When the waitress brought our food, Don asked of her with his winning smile, "Do you suppose you could do something for me?"

The waitress said, "Sure."

"Could you bring some plain orange juice in a Margarita glass and rim it with salt?"

His eyes twinkled as the waitress set the beautiful goblet of orange juice before me. "That salt has a special meaning for me now," Don said, with a little secretive smile.

After breakfast I announced the need for another trip to the Ladies', while Don took care of the bill, and said that he would have another cigarette and make another phone call. I joined up with him and he said goodbye to all the workers and diners that we passed on the way out of the restaurant. He seemed extremely happy. He told me his plan as we walked to the car.

"Okay, here's what we can do. If you can take me to the bus station, I'll buy the ticket and rent a locker to put the stuff in. Then Monica can go into town when her friends are able to take her and get her things, pick up the ticket and go on up to San Diego."

I looked at my watch. "Sure, we can do that. My appointment isn't until 1:15. It's going on 11 now. That gives us lots of time. Maybe you could hang around while I see the doctor and then we could do something after the appointment. That is if you don't have other plans."

"No, I'm including you in all my plans from now on, that is if you'll let me."

We started on the 15 mile drive to the bus station, with Don asking me questions but nothing terribly personal. I told him that I'd lived in California before I married my second husband and moved to Wyoming. We had bought several properties, some of which I still owned as Tenants in Common with my ex. Among them was 80 acres on a mountain that I had thought would make a good dude ranch. My ex had shuddered at the word "dude". I told Don I would love to get rid of that property but my ex had made it difficult. He was very stubborn about the idea but lately I thought he might be changing his tune, now that he realized that he was never going to do anything with it.

"When that marriage ended I moved to Las Vegas."

"I've got some friends there. Why did you move here?"

"I had a house there that my ex and I bought to have a place to spend some time in the winters. When we split up, I took that place as part of my assets and lived there for close to two years. Then when the house next door to my daughter came up for sale, I bought it and moved here. A friend of mine lived in the house in Nevada until about two years ago and I decided to sell it just last year. I still have some good friends there so I go to visit."

"Maybe we could go there sometime—to visit my friends

and yours and I've played a little poker at the casino there. I could do that maybe while you did your thing. We could stop in Las Vegas on our way and I could do some gambling. It's mostly all guys but if I could walk in with you on my arm—I'd feel like a king!"

"Well, believe me I'd have plenty to keep me busy while you were gambling. I love The Bellagio for the art gallery and conservatory and I've got some friends in Vegas too. Then we could meet up to listen to my favorite saxophone player who is at The Tuscany. We could stay at one of the resorts that I belong to. They have three and I like the one on the south Strip the best."

"This will be great! Don said. "Traveling with you and seeing all these places, some I've seen before but now it's like seeing everything for the first time." He seemed very excited.

Don was quiet for a while and then he asked, "If I'm not being too forward, can I ask what broke you and your husband up?"

"It was irreconcilable differences. He thought a woman wasn't worth much. I knew I was."

Having been a real estate broker, we had accumulated a lot of assets. We did a property split. I told Don that I took as part of my share the house in Nevada and I lived there in the winter, with my little dog Porky. Then my ex came and got her and took her back to Wyoming. We had bought several rental houses and the 80 acres of bare land, next to the forest.

We arrived at the bus station. I parked in the spot indicated by the sign and got out and opened the trunk. Apparently Don had called ahead or knew how things operated at the bus stations, for him to know that he could leave things in a locker there. He started to take all the things out of the trunk and manipulate how he was going to manage all of it.

"Here, I can help carry something."

"That's okay, I can get it," he protested.

"Don't be silly." I pulled the two and a half foot cylindrical thing out and closed the trunk.

We went into the bus station and over to the desk and Don set down the two large back packs and the other cylinder. I set the one I was holding down on the counter. The attendant took everything into a back room, after giving Don what I assumed was a claim check for everything. Then Don proceeded to buy a ticket. Not wanting to appear nosey, I strolled away and over to the window to check out some notices posted there.

"There! I'm glad that's taken care of. Now I'll let Monica know where she can get her stuff."

"So what do you think about waiting for me while I do the doctor's visit?"

"Sure, then we can figure out what we want to do later."

"Yeah, there's that karaoke thing that starts at seven or Sandi has a music thing at the Desert Hideaway that I haven't been to yet. She was just telling me about it on Friday. We could go back up there. It starts at sundown."

"Yeah, maybe so."

"On our way back to the doctor's office, we can stop by my place and I'll show you my chicken collection."

"You collect chickens?"

"Among many things."

I pulled into the driveway of my house. Don exclaimed over my patio which is quite large and has a lot of plants and furniture on it. I pointed out the dove's nest in a basket which I had sitting high up on a shelf.

"Don't look straight at them," I cautioned Don, "I don't want to upset Mama Dove,"

Inside I showed him my collection of all sorts of chickens and roosters.

"I should say you have got a collection here."

I told him I had counted them on a video tape I made, telling the story and origin of each one. It was something like 266, in my kitchen and breakfast room.

I pointed out various ones, telling him, "This one is from Venice, this one is from Iceland. This egg scale is an antique and it really works."

Then I showed him various rooms in the house, with a collection of different things in each one; butterflies in the guest room, where I pointed out various things that had once belonged to Dr. Papanicolau, the developer of the Pap smear for women. Briefly I told him the quick story behind my acquisition of them. He paused at my collection of birds commenting about the hanging I have of 16 individual stuffed cloth birds, hanging on a rope of beads with a bell on the bottom. He said he liked that. Then I showed him my prized collection of Indian art and artifacts. I told him about my first visit to Monument Valley and of our encounter with Floyd, a Navajo native who lived there.

Floyd and his cousin, a native also but an albino, were standing with their horses on a bridge which crossed a small rivulet of water. My family and I were driving through in the huge motor home that Sam, my fiance had rented for the occasion. Floyd asked us if we wanted a tour of the real Monument Valley, which tourists never get to see. We were thrilled at the chance. We piled into his pickup truck, with the younger ones sitting in the bed in the back. Floyd took us to his hogan, where he lived with his parents and two sisters. They all had a craft which they were busily working on. Floyd showed us where they slept inside the hogan, in a circle, with their bedding on the dirt floor. He invited us to come back and stay with them. I corresponded with Floyd for a few years and then lost touch. But he had kindled the fires within me to find out more about the Indian culture and so I had gone back to many places to learn more about the natives and I had bought souvenirs. I told Don each one had a story but we didn't have enough time for me to go into it. I would do so later. He was interested in two little antique dolls that I had. I told him they were very old. I also told him that one of my ancestors had been on the Trail of Tears. He seemed familiar with that when he asked me where it had originated. He seemed to be interested in everything in my house but then it would have been impolite of him to act in any other way.

I offered him something to drink, but he declined. He did say if I didn't mind that he would go outside and have a smoke before we headed out. I said, okay, that would give me a chance to set up the DVD player and show him the tape of Christmas in Wyoming on the 80 acre hilltop.

We watched the segment which shows my family and friends riding up to the gorgeous hilltop in snow machines and then us having a picnic, roasting steaks over a campfire surrounded by trees with gorgeous San Diegos of the valley below. The kids are taking sled rides, pulled by the Ex, riding a snow machine. Everybody is having fun and laughing.

"So, what do you think? Do you know anybody who might like to buy the place?"

"My kids will buy it!" Don declared.

Suddenly I saw a glimmer of hope that I might be able to get rid of this property that needed to be sold.

I pulled up at the gynecologist's office about 15 minutes early. I thought perhaps if I were early they might hurry things up so I could be free for the rest of the afternoon. This was supposed to be a routine visit, although I had noticed a little irritation and I wanted to get a prescription for Clotrimazole which had been prescribed for me three years before when I had a terribly stubborn and confusing yeast infection. At that time the doctor told me that I had him puzzled because nothing that they prescribed had any effect on my condition and in fact made it worse. Tests showed nothing. This had persisted for two months and finally, the only thing that helped was the Clotrimazole.

At the doctor's office there was an outer courtyard and inside two rather large waiting rooms. Don said that he would sit in the outer one so he could smoke. When I was at my house I had picked up the first two chapters from two of the books I was working on—one was what I had described to Don as a trashy romance and the other was a mystery based on a real-life experience. It dealt with a stalker.

When I had told Don previously about the "trashy romance" he said, "When you go into my place you'll find some cooking manuals and the rest is all trashy romance novels."

I had put these things in a manila folder and grabbed it from the back seat, along with a little book about the stupidest things people had ever done. I handed the folder to Don.

Don sat down on a bench-like seat in the courtyard with reading material in hand while I checked in at the desk inside.

Things took forever. One hour had passed and still I had not been seen by anyone. From where I sat in the waiting room I could observe Don reading the pages I had given him, and smoking. I also saw him talking on his cell phone at various times. Surely they would call me soon. Don finished reading the chapters and turned to the little book. Smiling, he would speak to people as they came and went from the inner office.

Finally the assistant took me in to get my weight and blood pressure which was reading higher than normal. I told her that was probably due to the extremely long time I'd had to wait. She told me to go back and have a seat and they would be calling me soon. I waited another 15 minutes and then Don was coming in the door. He needed to use the Men's room.

He handed me the folder and the book. When he came out I motioned for him to come over to the side of the room where I sat.

"Don sat down and said, "You're not pregnant are you? I noticed that all these women are pregnant."

I laughed. "No but this IS an OB/GYN office. You should sit in here, where it's cool. You can always go out to smoke when you need to. I don't know how much longer I'll be. I'm really sorry about this. I had no idea it would take this long. It never has before."

"Don't worry about it. I might need to get to a store before long though. Maybe I'll walk across the highway to a convenience."

"Take my car. I'm sure this is going to take quite a while longer—I haven't even seen the doctor yet."

"Oh, no, I can walk," he protested.

"No, really!"

"Are you sure?"

"Yes, go ahead." I felt really awful that this unexpected delay had happened.

"I'll be right back then," he said.

I handed him the keys. I thought maybe he had smoked all his cigarettes and needed to get some more.

When he came back he came into the waiting room and said, "That is a great little car! Drives nice and as you said, it gets great mileage. just what you need. That was a smart move on your part."

"Yeah, but it doesn't have power windows." I laughed because I had told him on Sunday that when I bought it I was desperate to get something I could depend on, when the two cars I had were undependable. The Infiniti SUV was falling apart, literally and the A/C didn't work in it very well nor in the black Jaguar that sat in my garage, failing to start without a jump. I said that I wanted something cheap with a good A/C that got good mileage and that this Fiesta got 40 mpg. I had failed to notice that it had wind up windows until I drove it off the lot and got it home.

While waiting Don and I sat talking about many things. Among them the possibility of going to San Diego so I could meet his family and then on up to Carlsbad to see my friends. His son was getting his motor home ready for him to come up so we could drive it to the coast and hook up my little car behind it. Don went out to smoke some more. I noticed him talking to one of the men who had accompanied his pregnant partner. Don asked him something and the guy came in and said something to his partner in Spanish. I couldn't make out what they were saying but I thought it might be about someplace that had music. The guy then went back outside and said something to Don.

I went in to the inner office and checked to see how much longer it would be. I was told "30 minutes," there were two people before me. I sat and counted as various people came and went hoping that they were my predecessors. After half an hour had passed I went back in to the inner outer office to check on the progress. They didn't know how much longer.

"Well, I have another appointment so I'll only be able to wait another 15 minutes or so." I showed my disgust. She told me she'd see what she could do. Soon I was ushered into the examining room and told to strip from the waist down.

It turned out to be a P/A that saw me and she informed me that I had "a lot going on down there." She proceeded to tell me in technical terms what it was. She asked me if I was allergic to any medications. I told her Premarin. She said that she was prescribing two things for me and told me what the side effects were. I was to see how the things worked and then she would call in a refill prescription because it was a two week course of treatment. She said my condition was pretty bad and she was surprised that I hadn't had more pain from it. I explained that I have a very high tolerance for pain and maybe that was the reason I had noticed only mild discomfort. I also told her that I was thinking of going over to the San Diego area for a couple of days, I wasn't sure when, but that I might not be home a week from then to get the other prescription. Could she order them both now? She said she would. Then I asked her what about drinking alcohol? She said there wasn't anything in the medication that should be interfered with by having a cocktail. Then I asked, "What about men?"

"No! You shouldn't have any intimacy with a man until the doctor has a chance to examine you and check this small questionable patch."

"Ordinarily that would not be a problem," I told her, "but I've just met a new friend and that possibility might be in the future."

"No. Doctor's orders are that you have no intimate contact until after everything is cleared up."

I nodded. "Now, how worried should I be over the patch you mentioned?"

"Don't let it ruin your life. Usually these things turn out to be nothing but anytime we note that there's an isolated area of this sort of thing we want to do a biopsy. I'll confer with the doctor to make certain but I'm sure she will want to do a biopsy on it."

I got dressed while the P/A called the prescriptions in and checked with the doctor. When she came back in the room she said yes, that they wanted to do a biopsy in four weeks.

This would change my plans for beginning a relationship. I would have to tell Don.

"Don, I have to go pick up my prescriptions. You should know what the doctor said as far as our beginning a new relationship which may involve intimacy. There can't be any of that. I have to begin this medication and take it for two weeks. They'll see if I'm healed at that time. Then they want me back in two weeks after that for a biopsy. The P/A said that I shouldn't worry too much but it's hard not to."

"Oh, I understand. All I want is to be with you. I can wait forever if I need to." He winked, "Well, I think I can. You just get better. I'm so head over heels about you, I just want to be with you. I can't believe I've found you. I can't believe you're for real. Let's go drop off your prescription and find a place to get something to eat. You're probably hungry."

"I guess the music at Sandi's will have to wait," I said ruefully.

"Yeah, we can do that another time. Actually it's the deadest of all the music venues up there. You may not even want to go. Tammy, said to check out two places in town, The Owl and Hailey's. Both are on Main Street and supposed to have music."

"We could check out karaoke at Sunshine Lake and then I can take you home. Let's find someplace for dinner."

In the restaurant Don was friendly as he always was, no matter where we went. He was very charismatic. The hostess paid special attention to us and then the waitress did the same. We each had a vodka and diet coke, my usual drink. Don said he quite liked it. I ordered what the hostess had suggested, which was chicken & shrimp in a cream sauce. Don ordered a steak with two baked potatoes, rather than a vegetable. I made a mental note of his poor eating habits along with the fact that he was lactose intolerant and smoked a lot and drank extremely strong black coffee.

Then the hour was up that the clerk had told us it would take to get the prescription filled. I stood in line and it had been a total of a little over an hour when my turn came and the clerk said that it was going to be half an hour more.

"But you told me . . ." I began.

Don touched my arm and said, "Let me. Look, you told us an hour. We went and had dinner and now you're telling us it's going to be another half hour. What's going on here? What's it going to be?"

Just then the manager of that department came over and asked what the problem was. Don was visibly upset. He told her.

She said, "No, it's ready just hold on a minute." She got the prescription, bagged it and apologized for the inconvenience.

After I paid and we were walking away I said, "How did you do that?"

Don said, "You just have to be firm. I'm an expediter-been doing it all my life. I see a problem and I fix it. You don't have to act angry or fly off the handle, but just assert yourself."

I really appreciated this quality in Don.

"Another thing, I noticed that you paid for the prescription. You don't have coverage?"

"Not for prescriptions. But I don't buy much medicine."

"Well, I can tell you how to fix that."

"How?"

"I'll have Tammy put you on the company's medical plan. I'll call her tomorrow."

We drove out to Sunshine Lake and drove around looking for the karaoke place. The music was supposed to begin at 7:00 p.m. It was close to eight by the time we found the place and walked up to the door. A man met us at the door and I asked if this was where the karaoke was.

He said, "Yes, but it's over."

"Over? But it only started at seven!"

"Yeah, that's right but everybody sang that wanted to and now everybody's gone."

He told us to come back another time.

Don and I laughed about it. We strolled around the grounds and looked at the moon. Don remarked about what a beautiful place this was and what a nice night and how lucky he was to be with this beautiful person. We got back in the car and decided to drive into town and try to find a place where we could listen to music and dance. I had brought out two CD's that I had compiled of Country Western music and I put one in the player. Every song that came on Don would rhapsodize over, saying "Oh I love this."

I told him I liked the old Country Western and had made these copies using only cassettes with songs that I loved too. I told him that my grandpa and aunts and uncles had all been musical, that they'd had barn dances in Kansas when my mom was young.

We drove on until I came to The Owl Café. It was dark. Don jumped out and peered in the windows. It was locked up tighter than a drum. I thought it might have been closed for good. So I drove on to the next place which was just down the street. I pulled up in front and Don said, "I'll check it out." He went up and looked in the windows. Back at the car he said, "I don't know about this place, I don't know if you'll want to go in there. See what you think."

I took one look and decided not. "Well, I don't know anyplace else to go. We could go to my house for a while and listen to my records and CD's."

And so that's what we decided to do.

I turned on my lava lamp. I turned on the skull which was illuminated by a bulb beneath, the one my brother Tommy had given me in November. I turned on the Himalayan Rock Crystal lamp which puts negative ions into the air which are supposed to be a cleansing tool. We had a drink, which was probably poor judgment on my part because I'd already had one at Applebee's. I put the first cassette in the player and we sat listening to the music. Don remarked about how nice this all was. Then he stood up and took my hand. "Dance with me."

We danced for a while, I drank some of my drink and then I knew I wasn't going to be able to drive him home. I told him, "You're going to have to stay here tonight because I'm in no condition to drive. But you have to understand that you'll stay in the guest room and we can't let anything happen."

"No, I understand that. I'm okay with it. Well, I'm not going to say it won't bother me. Sure, I'd like for it to go farther but I understand. I just want to hold you and be near you. That's all I want."

Black Velvet was playing and we were dancing a very sexy, slinky sort of dance. Don said, "Oh my God! Where'd you ever learn to dance like this?"

We kissed and stayed more or less in one spot in my hall which has a wall mirror and I could faintly see Don's hands running over my back and down my sides. I broke away from him.

"I know, I know, I promised, but, oh my God!"

I moved away from him.

"Just promise me one thing," he said as he caught me by the hand.

"What?" I asked him playfully.

"That this will be 'our song' and that when you're well, we can dance to this again."

"I promise." I kissed him softly.

We danced until 1:30 a.m. Then I showed Don where the fresh towels were and told him to make himself at home. I said goodnight and went into my room and locked the door behind me.

It was six am, as my illuminated watch told me. Still dark. Something had wakened me. I thought I could smell coffee. I grabbed my robe and slipped into it as I went out to the kitchen where Don was busily preparing breakfast. He had two plates with sliced apples on them. He was whisking eggs in a bowl and in a skillet was cooking some leeks. I had told him I liked leeks and scrambled eggs. He had found some English muffins and was buttering them. The coffee pot was almost empty.

"Here, I'll make some more coffee. I've drunk about all of that."

"How long have you been up?"

"Oh about 4:30. I made coffee and went out on the patio to smoke."

"I'm sorry. I didn't show you where the regular coffee is. You've been drinking decaf. That didn't give you much of a jolt, did it?"

Don laughed. "No, but I was jazzed already after last night."

"It must have been cold out on the patio."

"Yeah, but I had my memories to keep me warm Besides, I used a black jacket that I found in your closet. I hope that was okay?"

"Sure! Of course."

"Oh and look here," he pointed out the window to a dark thing that was hanging on the fence post. I could see that it was his black boxer shorts. "I washed those out and hung them out to dry."

"Oh, you're welcome to use the washer and dryer."

"No, that's okay. They'll dry in ten minutes in this desert heat. I will need to go to the store though, to get some things."

"I can take you up to the Desert Hideaway after we go to the bus station, so you can go to your trailer for some things and to see about the Chinese dinner."

"We'll see, maybe tomorrow. I may still go up there to serve the Chinese dinner. Tammy's supposed to be having food catered in and getting somebody to serve it. We'll see."

I poured the decaf in a warming pot and made a fresh pot of regular coffee for Don, while he scrambled first my eggs, which had milk mixed with them and then his, which did not. He had told me he was lactose intolerant.

"I didn't know where your toaster was kept so I just did the English muffins in the skillet."

"I'm sorry. I wasn't a very good hostess, leaving you to find everything for yourself."

"That's okay, you made up for it in other ways, but promise me something."

"Okay, what?"

"Promise me that you'll bring that CD that has Black Velvet on it and we can dance to it, again and again. C'mon Lady, sit down before your food gets cold."

I got the mugs of coffee and set them down at the table in the breakfast room, which he had set with silverware, napkins, salt and pepper. He asked me if I had a piece of scratch paper.

"Just a little scratch pad or something. I've started making a list in my head and I want to get it down on paper."

I went into the office to grab a couple of sheets of typing paper. When I handed them to Don, he hurriedly jotted down some things with his black and white pen.

As we were eating, we talked about when we might take some of our trips. Don was jotting things as we talked and ate.

When we finished I said I wanted to take a shower and Dontook his cup of coffee out to the patio, along with the sheet of paper.

After I was dressed and had put my make-up on and fixed my hair, I felt a lot better although I was still tired. But I had the burst of energy I always get when starting a new relationship. To me the thrill of finding out all about a new person was exhilarating. I could dance for hours, with very little sleep and be ready to go the next day.

I poured another cup of coffee and sat down across from Don, who was busy with his list.

"I talked to Tammy and she gave me some questions. Michael did too. But first, let's see what you think of this: We could do Germany in April sometime, maybe. And you said, you have a follow-up visit around the middle of March. Maybe we could go over to Las Vegas between now and then. We can go see your friends in San Diego or Carlsbad,. And then we'll look at taking a cruise later. Where would you like to go?"

"Oh, I'm open to suggestions. Where would you like to go? Where haven't you been?" I said.

"I've been on a lot. But to me it's the idea of cruising! Just to be with you on a ship—it doesn't matter where."

He showed me his list which had in large letters the word NAP. It was circled. He said that that was one of the first things he wanted to do today. Then he said, "Now Tammy has been working on this. She can't wait to meet you, by the way. She asked me, 'How long have you known Christina?' I told her a couple of hours and I knew. I reminded her that I met my wife on a Friday and married her on the following Monday and we were happily married for 43 years. Tammy remembers spoon-feeding me when I didn't have the will to go on when my wife died. She said to tell you 'Thank you.' Thank you for rescuing me."

I smiled at the thought of this gentle, loving man who seemed to be so totally engrossed with me.

"Now Tammy wanted me to ask, Are you okay with medical and/or prescriptions? With us putting you on the company's program?"

"I guess so." I didn't see how this would benefit me much as I took practically no prescribed medicine.

"Michael wanted me to ask if you want to sell your share of the 80 acres? The company can buy it and that would get you out from under it."

"Yes, but that would mean that you would be partners with the ex."

"That's okay, my kids have people who know how to work these things. They'd take care of it."

"The wiser thing to do might be to go to the ex with an offer. Let him decide if he wants to sell and let him approach me with the idea. He doesn't have to know I'm involved already. That way he can think it was his idea and satisfy his macho-man ego."

"Yeah, that's a good idea. We'll make him an offer, tell him it's a one-time cash offer, none of this counter offer crap. If he takes it, that's good. If he doesn't, you sell your half and we become his partner and deal with him."

Having worked with some big wheeler-dealers in my years in real estate, I was not put off by this suggestion and didn't think there was anything bizarre about it.

A couple of examples of situations that may have given me this mindset are:

1. A friend introduced me to a friend who said he wanted to invest in real estate in the U.S. He was a citizen of Mexico and wanted to buy apartment buildings here in the valley. I learned that he had on deposit upwards of three million dollars in U.S. banks, where he would deposit the $100,000 insurable at one bank by the FDIC. These were just the banks he chose to tell me about. He bought three apartment buildings from me and paid cash. Later he took me, along with

our mutual friend and his wife and the client's wife and small daughter on a driving tour all through Mexico as a show if appreciation to me for managing his properties. Because I had said I'd like to see the pyramids in Mexico he took me to Monte Alban. On the trip he pointed out various bridges and roads that he had built in Mexico and also the airline he had owned.

2. A man dressed in rather plain, somewhat shabby work clothes wandered into my office one day and said that he'd like to invest in real estate. He thought three of the smaller rental buildings that I showed him would work. His funds were coming from a lawsuit which had been settled, in which he had sued the utility company that had failed to oversee the levees that had flooded his marina and ruined his business. He bought the buildings for cash and I managed them for him.

3. A man came into my office looking for investments. He spoke very broken English, laden with a heavy accent. I asked him where he was from. He said LA now but he was from Yugoslavia originally. He had a very charming personality but I took everything he said with a grain of salt, thinking that the Mercedes he drove was probably rented. He didn't seem to have assets or the right answers. I thought nothing would ever come of it but I liked talking to him. He was funny, playful like a boy and he was trying so hard to seem like a big business man. He invited me to go to Marina del Rey to a function he was going to attend and to see his boat there. I did and we spent a nice Saturday afternoon together. Nothing romantic—just friendly. I got a call a couple of days later, wanting to

know if I could pick him and a friend of his up at the airport and show them some apartment buildings. I made arrangements and did this. The friend had flown them down in his private plane. It ended up by me making a sale to the friend for whom Destin had acted as a broker. Again the friend had access to cash so it was an easy sale. Destin did the leg work and made the connections. He didn't have any money himself but he had a knack for meeting friends, and forming a bond that enabled him to become partners with them or at least to broker deals for them.

I had learned to not form an opinion based solely on first appearances or first impressions. I had also learned to be observant and somewhat cautious with my natural exuberance and excitement when faced with new propositions. I trusted my instincts while others did not. Friends were aghast with what seemed to them to be risky behavior but I told myself that many of them would also have been aghast at my packing up my kids and driving off from Pittsburgh to Kansas or California to Pittsburgh. They would have been aghast too, at my grandmother who lived in a covered wagon in western Kansas in sub-zero temperatures while she was pregnant with her first child.

Also on John's list of items from Michael was that the motor home was being cleaned and stocked in preparation for our trip to San Diego on Sunday or Monday.

Don laid his sheet of paper aside and came around to my side of the breakfast table.

"I want to ask you something. I don't know quite how to put this. Sometimes I guess the best way is to just say it. He got down on one knee and took my hand in his and looked at me with the utmost sincerity. He seemed like the 19 year-old he was always saying he felt like.

"If the time is right and you want to . . .will you marry me?"

I was slightly amused at his serious look but I didn't want to insult him by laughing. I looked into his intense brown eyes and saw a deep longing. My eyes got misty. I said, "If it's right for you and right for me . . . yes!"

He looked elated. He grabbed me and hugged me. I really got teary eyed as I said to him, "This reminds me of a song, 'Something Good' from The Sound Of Music and the lines, 'Somewhere in my youth or childhood, I must have done something good.'"

"Okay. I've got to go out and smoke and call some people."

"And I'm going to call Jane and take my pill. I rushed into my bedroom, closing and locking the door behind me and on into the bathroom.

"Jane, Don just proposed to me."

"What???" You don't know him. You don't know anything about him. Where is he now?"

"He's on the patio, smoking and telephoning somebody."

I told her how he had done it, down on his knee and everything. She said how romantic that was. I told her that I had to talk fast and I quickly filled her in on things we had talked about. She had been trying to find out information about Don but hadn't been able to come up with anything using the names that she had to work with. This bothered her. I told her that we were coming up to her area in a few days and that she would have a chance to meet him.

Then I went back out to the kitchen. Don had come back inside and was standing by the island in the kitchen. He was on the phone too. I mouthed "Jane" and he said to tell her Don said hello. He mouthed "Tammy" and I said "Hi, Tammy."

Don said, "She says to tell you thank you and congratulations!"

Jane could hear some of what was going on. She said, "What'd he say?"

I said, "Here, say hello to Don."

They were talking about Don's motor home that had a deck on top, good for watching NASCAR. And the Rose Parade. I made a comment about seeing the races at Riverside. Then Don said that we could take the motor home to Oceanside where they had a "place" also, which was 'on the sand' and he would cook dinner for Jane and Rich, her husband. They seemed to have "places" all over and I had mentioned this in one of our many conversations, asking him if they were time-shares, like what I owned. He said, no, that they had acquired many properties through the years. He was simply a figure-head now. His sons and Tammy handled everything.

I went in to my computer and pulled up a song on You Tube. I went back and took the phone from Don. I said something about Don chasing me around the island or bed. Everybody laughed. Suddenly Don jumped up from the chair he was sitting on and burst out laughing. He hadn't realized when I handed him my phone, he had laid his cell phone in his lap so he could talk to Jane and now Tammy was yelling at him. He said goodbye to her and said, "Tammy reminded me to tell you congratulations and she can't wait to meet you."

"She didn't hear me when I said you were chasing me around the bed, did she?"

"Yeah, she did."

"Oh no! What did she say?"

"She wanted to know if I caught you." He winked.

"And did you also tell her that it wouldn't do you any good if you did catch me?"

"No. She doesn't need to know all our business."

We sat down and Don said, "Now I want to ask you something. Tammy is getting the house in San Diego ready for us to come over and look at it. I haven't gone back in it since Valerie died. It's kept just like it was before, with her musical instruments. She wrote songs, as I told you before. My sons are telling me we need to do something with the house-they're paying for all the upkeep and utilities on it for nothing. Now here's what I want to ask you; If we go there and you like it do you think you could live in the house after we're married?"

"That would depend on how you feel about it. I wouldn't be happy in a place where you weren't happy."

"I could be happy anywhere with you but I don't know if I'd want to live there or not with all those memories. Now, Tammy said that our realtor, who we stole from a we;;-known real estate company, to work solely for us on our properties, has a couple of comparable homes for us to look at. She said if we like one of those she wouldn't have any problem selling ours. You might like it, it's got a natural rock swimming pool and hot tub and big windows overlooking a gorgeous view. What's not to like? And if you find that that's where you want to be, then that's where we will stay. Simple as that."

"I'll repeat; I couldn't be happy if you were not."

I got up and told Don to come with me, I wanted to show him something. I went over to the computer. He stood behind me as Julie Andrews began singing Something Good. I sang along to bits of it. He stroked my hair and shoulders as Christopher Plummer and Julie Andrews sang the duet part.

"That is beautiful. You're beautiful," he murmured against my hair.

I played some of my quizzes on the computer with Don remarking how smart I was. "I didn't know the answers to any of those questions."

"Well, I was lucky today."

I went in and began taking dishes out of the dishwasher while Don began putting them away. I didn't say anything when he put them in the wrong place. He came up behind me as I reached down to get a spoon that had fallen into the bottom of the dishwasher.

"Oh, aren't dishwashers wonderful? he said as he moved up behind me and rubbed against me.

"You are a naughty boy," I said as I smacked his hand.

"I know, I know, just let me stand here for a minute. Oops, don't you need to bend over a little bit to get that thing down there?"

I laughed and said, "You know you're just making it worse for both of us."

"Yes, I know. I can't help it. I'm going out to smoke and then maybe I'll take a nap."

When he came back in the house he said, "Okay, Tammy told me that Monica wasn't going up there or she doesn't think she is today. So, I'm going to have to go in and pay for another day at the bus station for the storage. Do you think we can go there and maybe I could stop at a department store? And we could get something for dinner. What would you like me to cook for you?"

"Sure we can go there. Maybe you need to take a nap first."

It had been close to four hours since I took the medication which was supposed to last for a week. It was a time-release capsule and I was beginning to feel very nauseated. I told Don and also that I probably wouldn't be able to sleep. I found it very difficult to sleep in the daytime. Don offered to help me with the application of the vaginal cream, saying that his wife Valerie had suffered from yeast infections and that he had helped her insert the cream. He said this in a half joking manner. I really didn't feel much like joking or any of his innuendos right then. I just shook my head no. He asked if he could just lie on the bed beside me, that he wouldn't bother me. So I lay down and covered myself with a throw because I felt chilly in spite of the warm temperature while he lay on the other side of the king-sized bed and pulled one of the pillows over his eyes.

He fell asleep quickly but not before he murmured, "This is nice. So nice."

The extreme nausea passed after about 20 minutes. When Don woke up we went into town, first to the bus station. Don had told me that he needed to get something that belonged to him out of the backpack. When I pulled into the driveway of the station he said, "Why don't you pull over to the shade and park there and I'll just run in fast and pay them?"

I wasn't feeling 100% so that was okay with me. I closed my eyes and relaxed.

When Don came out he said, "I almost forgot this. The guy said 'do you need to get anything from the bags?' and I said, "Oh yeah!" He held up a small dark case.

From there I drove over to the second-hand store. Don said he wanted to pick up a pair of pants. This didn't bother me as it might some. I often frequented second-hand stores. My daughter and I go to the second-hand in San Jose every time I'm up there. I did caution Don that our store had a very meager selection and that proved to be true. He couldn't find anything. I had told him earlier at my house that he didn't need to shiver in the cold and I handed him a new pair of black sweat pants that my ex husband had bought but never wore.

On the way out of the store I spied some new bejeweled spike heels, covered with brocade and fake gems, still in the box. I said, "Ooohh!"

Don said, "Do you like those? Suppose they have your size?"

I searched and found a 7 ½ and was surprised at how comfortable they were.

Don eyed them and said, "Oh yeah! We need those shoes!"

On the way out he told me when I was better that we would go out dancing and I should wear the shoes.

I laughed and said, "Yes! We'll be stylin'"

From there Don wanted to go by a tobacco shop he had seen on the way over to the second-hand. We found the place and he ran in and quickly out again.

"Nope, wasn't the right kind of tobacco shop."

It seems it was the kind people went into and smoked those hookah (?) pipes. Then I was headed for the department store when I remembered I wanted to show Don the house I had lived in previously, before I got married and moved away to Wyoming. So I turned around and drove up the street and past the house, pointing it out to Don. Then I drove past the two real estate offices I had had on this end of town. I was starting to feel very nauseated again.

"What do you think you might want for dinner?" Don asked me.

"You know, I'm feeling a little sick. I don't know if I can eat."

Just then we passed a KFC and I said, "On second thought I might like to have a couple of wings."

"Sure," Don said. "Pull in there and I'll get them for you."

After asking what I wanted for side dishes, he went in. I was growing more nauseated as the time passed. When he came out I said we'd better hurry along and go to the little food store. We had gotten a little way down the road and I asked him what he'd gotten for himself.

He said, "I didn't want to tell you this because you'd probably make me go back but I ordered a breast for myself and paid for everything. Then the girl said that it would be 20 minutes, that a new batch was cooking. I said I didn't want to wait because I knew you were feeling sick. She said I could take the barbeque or extra spicy that was ready now. I told her I didn't want those, I wanted Original."

"So what did you get?"

"Nothing."

"Oh no, that's not going to fly with me."

"It's okay, I'll get something at the little food store for me."

"Well, you can just help me eat whatever you got for me. I don't have much of an appetite."

We went to the little food store. I told Don this was my favorite store and so much so that my daughter had given me two gift cards for 100 dollars each. I was feeling a little better as we walked through the store. Don wanted to get some razors, some mouthwash (I had only a little bit at home) and something for dinner and for the next day's breakfast. We bought four bananas, picking out the barely ripe ones, which Don and I agreed were the only ones to buy. He got some ham, bagels, powdered sugar doughnuts (I grimaced at the thought of those) a bunch of asparagus, a quart of milk, a dozen eggs for, as he reminded me, he had used all the eggs I had, for breakfast. When we got in line to check out I asked him to go back and find some Ritz crackers, thinking that these might settle my stomach. He came up and got ready to pay the cashier.

"No, you are not going to do this. You've paid for everything and I'm eating this food too so I need to use my gift card."

When we left the store he remarked, "I can't believe that I'm letting you pay for this."

When we got home, there was a message on my machine. I listened to it and the person or persons hadn't waited for my quirky message to complete its greeting so it wasn't clear when he left a message. It started by saying, "She hung up!" But then I heard what sounded like Clarence's voice telling him to write the number down. I called Don in to listen to it.

"I think this sounds like Clarence. Maybe he needs to talk to you about the Chinese dinner."

Don shrugged and acted like he didn't care about it. I told him I thought he should call Clarence because I was sure the people were wondering what was going on with the dinner. So he called Clarence. I heard his side of the conversation, "Yes sir. Yes sir! And then he listened to what Clarence was saying. I had busied myself with getting my plate ready with the chicken. Don went to the kitchen and began to toast an English muffin and make himself a sandwich.

"What did Clarence want?" I asked him.

"He wanted to tell me that I left the door of my trailer unlocked, so he went over and locked it. Also he said the people were wondering about the dinner and I told him my kids were taking care of it. Maybe you and I could go up tomorrow and serve the thing?"

"Sure," I said. But I don't think I'm going anywhere tonight. I'm starting to feel really sick."

"Well, come on Honey, sit down and eat something, maybe you'll feel better."

I turned the TV on and tried to eat a chicken wing but couldn't get it down. I ate some of the mashed potatoes and they were a little more palatable. I offered some of the chicken to Don but he said he was okay with the sandwich he had made. I decided to save my food in the fridge for the following day. Surely I would feel better then. I apologized to Don, saying that I was sorry to be such a wet blanket. I hardly ever got sick. It must be the medication that the doctor had prescribed and maybe I was allergic to it. Don told me not to worry about it. We could go to bed early because he was tired too, after the night before and then getting up so early. Some sleep would do us both good. If it wouldn't bother me, maybe he could lie with me and watch a little TV and then when I fell asleep he would shut the TV off and go into the guest room.

I put a Perry Mason DVD in the player. I joked that, "I go to bed with Perry Mason just about every night."

I awoke at 9:00 o'clock, feeling the need to vomit. Don had left the nest and the TV was turned off and the door was closed. I threw up for the first time and still felt ill. I was up again in another hour and a total of five times before I stopped retching. I vowed that I would call the doctor in the morning. I slept better and in the morning, in the darkness, I heard a soft rapping on my door.

"Are you awake"

"Yes? Come in."

Don opened the door. "How are you feeling?" He sat on the edge of the bed.

"Better," I told him.

"Good, I just wanted to come in and see how you were and if you feel like you want breakfast. I was outside and man! Is it cold out there!"

"Come here," I said as I flipped the covers down on the opposite side of the bed.

Don crawled into the bed and nestled up to me. I could feel that he was cold. I pulled his body closer to mine and we snuggled there.

He said, "I showered and washed my hair and used the mouthwash so I wouldn't smell like cigarettes."

"You're fine," I murmured sleepily.

"I know we can't do anything but can we just lie here close? Can I just hold you?"

"Un huh," I agreed.

He murmured as he kissed my neck, "This is so nice. So

great." He ran his hands over my body which was covered by my nightgown. He didn't attempt to raise the gown or get any more intimate than just the touching of my body through the fabric.

"I know I promised you and I won't do anything more but you know that it's killing me, right?"

"I'm sorry."

He turned my face to his and kissed me, not passionately but sweetly.

"Someday soon," he breathed as he kissed my neck.

Then he asked, "What can I fix you for breakfast?"

"I had such a miserable night, I think I'll just have an apple. I'm going to call the doctor. I think maybe I'm allergic to the medication."

"Okay, there's been a change of plans. Last night I talked to Tammy and she said that Monica had gone on over to San Diego. Tammy and my son are really mad at Monica. They don't want to deal with it. I guess I'll have to do something with her things. Now they want us to come over there, so they can meet you. Do you think we could go today?"

I was feeling much better and thought maybe all the effects of the medication were out of my system so I told Don I didn't see why not.

I got up and went to the living room to watch the news, sitting in my chair while Don sat on the couch opposite me.

"Okay, let me tell you my plan and see what you think."

Then Don began to outline what he thought our course of action should be for our future. "I know that you like to spend time with your daughter and I like to go back and forth to see my sons, so I think we should make this our home base, to come to in between our trips around California and elsewhere. We will need to have an income in addition to what we now have—to do all we want to do. For that reason I would like to look for property to build or renovate and open a restaurant/ supper club type business that has music and dancing. You know how hard it was for us to find someplace and I'll bet there would be a good market for something like that. What do you think?"

"I don't know about that. It seems that the market here is with a younger crowd where they can go and sing, or watch sports. The chain restaurants and Mexican restaurants do okay but I don't know about a dancing place. And I'm sure you realize that a restaurant is the hardest thing to keep going."

"Yes it is and for this reason, when they go into the restaurant business they have a big overhead, of rent for the building. That's a big nut to crack. When my sons and I open a place we pay cash for the building, that eliminates the huge rent factor to overcome. Then, and I've done this before, we offer a really big deal to promote the place, to get it started. A 55 cent breakfast. Where can you get a breakfast for 55 cents?"

"And how can you make money on it?" I wanted to know.

"We did this on a restaurant about 10 years ago. Eggs were five cents apiece. Toast maybe another 10 cents. Hash browns were practically nothing because we bought in huge bulk from Cisco. So we're looking at a 50/50 breakfast. But, we offer on the side at a price, a big, very thin slice of ham or a big slice, very thin mind you, of sirloin. People buy with their eyes. They see this huge slice of meat, no matter how thin it is, it makes them feel like they've got a bargain. Coffee, milk, everything is extra. The 55 cent deal brings them in and the extras pay the bills. Then they start coming in for lunch and dinner and if you've got dancing in the evening, they'll stay for that plus drinks and snacks. I can make soups like my recipes for that famous restaurant I told you about. Those are all my recipes that they use. He had told me of his connection early on and

I had tried to find some mention of it and couldn't. Neither could Jane.

"Now the thing is, I'll want to put this in your name. I'm old, I'm not going to be around forever and I'd want you to have something for after I'm gone."

"It sounds like you know what you're talking about and you've got a track record."

"Yeah, I've put some deals together and some people might say I was ruthless about some things but I never cheated anybody. We'd get the places up and running and advertise heavily with the Asians. They buy the place and can't make a go of it but that's not our fault. I've also done some good things for people along the way like the time I was working for a large hotel chain and would go into places to oversee how the operation was going. In this one place I saw the manager mistreating his employees, bawling a waitress out for something that wasn't her fault.

"So I went up to him and said, 'Get your things and get out!'

"He said,' Who do you think you are? You can't come in here and fire me!'

"Then I told him who I was and why I was there and he said, 'Oh I guess you can do that.'

"He promised not to do it again and apologized to the waitress so he didn't lose his job. I just don't like to see the underdog get a raw deal."

I had sat spellbound listening to his plans for a business then I got an idea. "Yes, and maybe my son-in-law could work as a chef in the operation. This is what he did before, until his boss got flaky. He might like to do that again."

"Sure thing! Now tell me, can you recommend a realtor, so I can go look at some buildings?"

"I'm completely out of the loop. I did have a conversation

with one gal who was going to invite me to go to the real estate meetings with her. She never called me."

He frowned. "Well, we definitely won't be calling her."

I handed him the phone book.

"Now tell me one more thing, "I'd like to buy you a ring. May I? If you don't want to wear it you don't have to, I just want to buy you one."

"Well, of course I would wear it."

"Good. I'm going to call some agents and make appointments. How long do you think it will take you to get ready to go to San Diego?"

"Probably two to three hours. I've got to wash my hair and call the doctor about this dumb medication that's making me sick."

"O.K. That'll give me time to look at some properties and then we can head for San Diego."

It was about 7:30 a.m. when he started making his phone calls. He had asked to use my cell phone because his was dead. We tried to use my charger but it didn't fit. I told him no one would be in the office that early. He said he was calling them at home. If they wanted to make a sale, they would work with him. I heard him talking to one guy who told him he very seldom went into the office, that he worked out of his house but this morning he had wanted to get away from the kids and have a cup of coffee, so he would meet Don at his office at 9:00 a.m.

I called my daughter Kim to see if she wanted to meet Don, since we might be leaving for San Diego later that day and would be gone for several days. She was too busy, trying to get off to work and dealing with her dying dog, Gracie, so she didn't want us to go over to have her meet Don.

Don made other phone calls and made little notations on

a piece of scrap paper. He asked what my phone number was so he could leave a message for agents to call him back.

About 8:30 he said, "I should be going. I'll let you know how it's coming along. I'll change into the sweats when I get back and then we'll go over to San Diego so you can meet the kids."

"Don, you take the car. I have a lot to do to get ready. I need to pack for several days and get the house ready to leave."

"Oh, I thought you'd just drop me off and I could walk to these offices."

"No, you go ahead. I trust you."

"You trust me . . ." he smiled.

Don called me a little after 8:30 a.m. . "Well that agent was a big waste of time. How's the packing coming along?"

"Yes, I'm nearly all packed. I called the doctor. She said that I shouldn't take any more of the medicine. I'm feeling better today. I think I'll be okay to travel."

"Good! There's been a change in plans. Michael and Tammy have to go to Phoenix and want to stop by your place on their way through."

"Oh no! My house is filthy!"

"Oh, it is not. Your house is beautiful. Well they really want to meet you and they won't get to because they'll be in Phoenix when we're in San Diego. We'll be staying with Kevin now. But only for a day or so because I don't want to be around them too much—it's too noisy with the kids and everything going on."

"What time will they get here?"

"I'm not sure. They said they were on the road already but they'll call me. They may even get there before I'm finished in town."

"And how will they find me? This isn't the easiest place in the world to find even with a GPS."

"They'll call me and I'll find out more details. I'll let you know. Bye Love."

I hurriedly straightened up my house in preparation for the guests who were going to pop in.

The phone rang at 11:30 and when I answered a woman's voice asked me, "Do you know a Don Peterson?"

"Yes, I do."

"Are you his wife?"

"No."

"Girlfriend?"

"Sort of."

"Well, this is Jackie Garcia and Don told me you're the love of his life. Can you get hold of him? I need to get a message to him."

"I just heard from him a little while ago and his phone is going dead so I'll have to wait until he calls me again."

"I spoke to Don and he wanted to look at the Boatwright's Bakery building for his project. He called me from the department store and wanted to look at it right now but I told him I had to call the owners and set up an appointment. We made an appointment for 2:00 p.m. I called the owners and was told that they've taken the property off the market so I need to tell Don that. When he calls you if you could give him that message and tell him that I'll look for other properties that might be suitable. Oh and he said that he was going to the clinic that's close by and have a procedure that would take about two hours."

"Procedure! What's the matter with him? Did he look sick to you? Did he act sick?"

Jackie said, "No, I didn't see him. I only spoke to him on the phone. He seemed a bit rushed, maybe. And he said to tell you that if you need your car in the meantime that it's parked in front of the clinic and the keys are inside."

"If I need my car? How does he think I'm going to get to town to get my car? That IS my ride!"

I thanked Jackie and hung up. Then my wheels started turning. What sort of procedure? What sort of clinic was it? Did he leave my car unlocked? The only way you can lock it is with the keyless entry. Did he hide my keys under the mat or what?"

I thought about this a little bit and called Jackie back. "What sort of clinic is it?"

"It's a dental clinic on one side and a medical clinic on the other."

"And you said he was leaving the keys inside. Inside what?"

"Inside the clinic."

I looked up numbers in the phone book for any clinics in town. There was a listing for a dental clinic on Main Street, not far from Jackie's office. There was no other clinic listed. I called the number and spoke with a receptionist. I asked her if someone had left some keys for me to pick up. She told me no. Then I asked her if they had treated a patient by the name of Don Peterson. She told me no and that all of their appointments had been before 11:00 a.m. They had no more for the rest of the day. I asked her if she could give me the number of the other clinic on the other side. She said, "Yes, I'll look it up."

I hung up and called the other number and asked the receptionist if someone had left keys for me.

"No." My heart sank. "Oh wait, let me ask the other girl."

Another person picked up the phone. "Yes, a man left keys for you and said you might be in to pick them up."

"Yes, well someone will be in to get them." I thanked her.

As far as I knew Don was still on his real estate quest and might be going back to get the car as soon as he found out he didn't have a two o'clock appointment.

I had called Jane to keep her apprised of what was happening. I told her different scenarios of what I thought possibly may have happened: that Don was still out looking at real estate: that he had called Jackie, found out that he couldn't see the property that he wanted to look at and had looked at something else: that his son and daughter-in-law had come into town and met up with him and they all had gone to look at whatever he had found: that he had gone to search for my engagement ring and couldn't call because his cell phone was dead. None of it made sense.

By my calculations and the sketchy information I'd gotten from Don, his kids could be arriving at my place, probably not before noon, but then, depending upon any stops they would make, if they stopped for breakfast and/or lunch or drove like maniacs, they could arrive at any time. As the time wore on and I heard nothing from Don, I was left to form more scenarios: maybe they had met up with Don and he went with them to see some other real estate with one of the other agents: maybe they were having lunch: maybe they had decided not to come to my house. My experience with high-rollers told me that there might be any number of bizarre scenarios here and this seemed to be the type of people I was involved with. Maybe Don hadn't heard any more from them and had gone about trying to find a ring for me. Is that why he was in the department store when he called Jackie? One of my many phone calls to Jane on this morning was to ask her if department stores sold engagement rings.

"Yeah, but that's a weird place to get one."

I had told her earlier that it looked like we might be coming to see her over the weekend now, rather than the following week.

Two o'clock came and went. I called Jackie.

Have you heard any more from Don?

"No."

"I haven't either."

I decided to wait until three o'clock before I called a cab to take me to get my car.

It was in a very busy medical clinic on Main Street that I retrieved my keys. They were in an envelope with my name written on the outside.

At three o'clock I had called the Yellow Taxi company and had them pick me up. I figured if Don showed up later he would just have to understand why I didn't want to leave my car any longer in front of the clinic. The driver called me back to verify where I lived. Even the professional drivers had a problem finding me, I told myself, so what chance would Don's family have? And for that matter, Don could have gotten lost too. When the driver pulled into my driveway I asked if I should sit in front? The driver nodded. I told him I was going to the clinic in the 600 block of Main Street. We had a nice conversation on the drive in to town, with him telling me about raising his teenaged son and trying to instill values in him. He seemed like a nice man. I didn't expect the fare to be $15.00, it was only three miles, and according to the chart, it should have been less. I had only $16.00 in cash. I apologized for the $1.00 tip. He seemed glad for the fare.

Driving home I was still wondering what had happened. I couldn't figure out what was going on. Don hadn't indicated in any way that he was a con artist. I went over everything he had told me, what his demeanor had been, what other people's reaction to him had been—everyone seemed to love him—about his cooking for the people, about his knowledge of how real estate transactions worked, of how the restaurant business worked, about places he had been and his knowledge in general about so many things.

At 6:00 p.m. the phone rang. My caller ID said 'Restricted'.

"Ma'am, This is the sheriff's department. Do you know a Don Peterson?"

My first thought was that Don had been in an accident.

"Yes, I know him."

"Do you know where he lives?

"He lives at the Desert Hideaway as far as I know. What's wrong?"

"Do you know how old he is?"

Now my thoughts turned to his being involved in a crime.

"No, I don't."

"Do you know where he is?"

"No, and you're frightening me. I live by myself. Do I have something to be afraid of?"

He told me no, it wasn't anything like that.

"No ma'am. It's nothing you need to be concerned with. Could you let us know if you do hear from him?"

"Sure. I do know somebody who may know more about him than I do. I'll try to call him and let you know." I verified the caller's name and telephone number and hung up.

Then the cell phone rang. I answered and it was the same deputy. I told him I had just spoken to him on my house phone and now he was calling my cell phone. He thanked me and hung up. Small town cops!

Then I called Clarence. "Have you heard from Don?" I asked.

"Who is this? Oh, Christina! No, I haven't heard from him but these people up here are real mad at him, the people from the Chinese dinner thing that he was supposed to have."

So that had to be it! This was the only connection between Don and me that would have had both my house phone number and the cell phone number and then the deputy telling me that, "It's not anything like that" re-enforced my thought that it had to be the Chinese dinner gone wrong. I tried to call the sheriff's deputy but couldn't make the right connection.

I called Jane and told her the sheriff's department was looking for Don. She listened, aghast at what I was telling her.

"But why? Why this elaborate story?" she wondered.

She asked a question that we would be asking each other and others as the following days and weeks went by.

Then I called my daughter next door to tell her I wouldn't be going to San Diego. She told me she didn't want to get involved with men I had met, that I was being careless and why on Earth would I let him use my car when I didn't know him? I told her there were extenuating circumstances. She said it was dangerous and she didn't ever want to get involved with some of the people I was meeting. She said if I didn't start being smarter that she was going to send me to a nursing home. I said they would have to prove that I needed to be committed and they wouldn't be able to do something like that. I told her I wouldn't get her involved again.

Phone calls to and from my friend Jane were fast and furious. We both got busy on our computers, trying to find out who Don Peterson was. Jane asked me to call her first thing in the morning. when I woke up. I made up my mind that I would begin to do some serious detective work, trying to find out who and what and why Don Peterson was.

I had remembered the video tape that I had made of Don and me, images that I took when I met him that Sunday when I went to the Desert Hideaway for breakfast. I almost went out to my garage to get it but the fact that I had already put on my pajamas for the night prevented me from doing that. That night I slept with all my lights on and a hammer under my pillow, my cell phone and house phone on the bed beside me and a can of wasp spray by the side of my bed, within easy reach.

The next morning I was afraid that my video camera in its case might be missing, that Don may have carried it off to wherever he had gone. I was relieved when I found it on the back seat of my car, where I had left it over two weeks ago. I brought it in and saw that the battery was working fine. I had thought that I had to shut it off at the Desert Hideaway because the battery needed charging and that I would do that in preparation for our trip to The Center Of The World. I turned the camera on and backed it up and saw the video I had taken of The Artist's Grotto.

But had I taken any shots of Don? Further backing up showed Don as he introduced himself to the camera. A mild man, shy with a gentle smile on his lips was speaking softly into the camera.

I would like to know if a psychological evaluation was ever done on Don and what the findings were. I'd like to know what made him into the pathological liar that I now believed him to be. What caused such low self-esteem? Was his life so barren that he lived in a perpetual make believe world, with the supporting actors changing to suit him?

Some people are now ready to paint a very dark picture of him but at the same time others tell me that he did a lot of good for people. They tell me of his cooking many meals for the people at the Desert Hideaway, without expecting anything in return. Did the fact that those same people falsely accusing him of stealing chairs and pots and pans from them make him feel justified in taking the $125.00 intended for the Chinese dinner?

Did the fact that I told him I trusted him prevent him from stealing my car, when he very easily could have done so? Did it compel him to leave instructions with Jackie to telephone me on how and where I could get the keys, instead of just abandoning it, leaving me to wonder where my car was? Perhaps it was the knowledge that I would have turned it in to the police and they would have searched for it and for him that stopped him from doing this. I loaned it to him. Twice. He had had two opportunities to take my car and run.

I'm reminded of inequalities in the thinking of individuals and in groups which arises out of prejudgment, prejudice and the disparity and injustice in our system and our society. I think about the time when I was a teenager, a juvenile delinquent having been sent to live with my aunt after I stole two cars. I mention this incident in the first chapter of this book.

After four months the probate judge traveled forty miles to evaluate my rehabilitation and consider the possibility of returning me to my family.

He took me to a nearby park, telling my aunt that he wanted to speak to me alone. He put his arm around me, comfortingly I thought at first. After all it was broad daylight in this little town in Kansas. He was a respected probate judge. I was a convicted felon. Then the respected judge proceeded to make a pass at me. I moved slightly away from him and ignored it and treated him as if nothing untoward had happened. This action could have been construed as completely innocent, at least in any version he might feel compelled to tell if he was ever questioned about it. I didn't want to mess up my chances of going home. But that would not include submitting to his advances. It didn't come to that. But I was facing two years of reporting to him on a weekly basis and who knows how many more possible passes or who knew what sort of contrivances the licentious, but supposedly fine and upstanding judge might dream up?

Solving the Riddle that was Don one year later. Or trying to.

In retrospect, I'm glad I took notes, for some of the details have diminished over the last several months. But my notes make it all come flooding back. I'm reminded of how I felt when I was with Don and what it felt like to have him take off and disappear without a word. I will refer to those notes while trying to figure the whole thing out, which I don't suppose I'll ever do. I can only guess at his motives, feelings and thoughts. I would like to know about his early life and later, his married life.

He was so utterly convincing in nearly everything he said and did. The very few slip-ups that he made in our early conversations could have been attributed to my not paying full attention. And there were only a few very minor ones. I've tried to figure out if he had told his story so many times that he believed his lies himself but I know that couldn't have been true of his conversation about real estate. He must have had a photographic memory to not have slipped up more. I have a very good memory for detail, inordinately so and I would have caught his discrepancies. He also had to have a high degree of intuition to know what would work with different women. And men. I've met some of these people and they are very intelligent. So it's not that Don preyed on people who were starved for affection or company. Perhaps they were open to a friendship that didn't follow the "normal" criteria; that is, being able to form a relationship in an unusual place like the Desert Hideaway. There is a vast majority of people who would never venture into a place like this. Some of them look at the inhabitants as dregs of society or as one man put it to me just recently, "lowlifes." There are others who are tired of society and it's boundaries, laws, criticisms, rules, regulations, much like the hippies of the Sixties. A good number of this type have elaborate motor homes, new cars and off-road vehicles. They dress well, eat well and many of them had successful careers before they took to the road, heading for campsites or temporary parks for the season, only to move on when weather or other reasons warranted the move. The reason for them leaving conventional society, choosing instead this seemingly nomadic type of existence, was only vaguely apparent to me, however I was to learn more in the upcoming weeks and months.

I was to meet quite a few of these people when my inquiring mind wanted to know what made Don tick. What drove him to concoct these elaborate scenarios for himself? Was it because he needed to adjust his made up life to fit his new surroundings and new people, while keeping some of his favorite details from the past? All the while he was further embellishing his new role. People would change in each new situation, presenting opportunities for development and enlargement that he could weave into a new scenario with variations to increase his role as actor and director. Was he trying to convince himself as well as those around him?

Then when he could see that in the near future, inevitably, his newly created world would come crashing around him, he had to move on to new horizons. He could go to this new environment where he could be king for a while. What a repertoire of situations he was creating for himself and for whomever he would encounter along the way! Most certainly they would have some experience to be added to his considerable stockpile. They would live in his make-believe world with him for a short time. He would glean bits from them and then move on. Possibly they would be saddened by his going. Perhaps Don might wish he could stay longer but no, his lies and make believe world would betray him. He must keep moving. Was he a pathological liar? Or a psychopath? Or both? I understood a psychopath to be violent, aggressive and/or anti-social. Don didn't exhibit any of these traits in the time I spent with him.

Was he trying to establish some self worth? Had his early life been so dismal that he needed to create a more fulfilling one in each brief encounter that came along?

He wasn't trying to bilk people for money. He wasn't a thief. He wasn't a rapist. He wasn't in it to get possessions. He had plenty of opportunity to commit all of the above and he didn't do any of those things, with the possible exception of stealing the Chinese dinner's $125.00. But from what one of the people I interviewed later said, they probably owed it to him. But I'm getting ahead of my story.

I did sleep Thursday night and when I awoke Friday morning I was determined to find out more about Don. I had two links to him, the bus bus station people and Clarence at the Desert Hideaway. And there were possibly more in the police and sheriff's departments. There were the real estate people he had contacted, how many I didn't know but I knew of two for sure; the one he had called from my cell phone, whose number was still in my phone and Jackie who had called me back to tell me about my car and to pass a message on to Don about their aborted appointment. Possibly there were others. I started making a timeline and made copious notes.

I called the bus station and the clerk, Alma told me that Don had bought a ticket for $27.50. I asked what buses they had leaving Thursday afternoon I was told one for San Diego (that made sense) and one for Los Angeles. But that one was $28.50, with a stop in Indio. I didn't know how bus lines worked. I thought possibly he had finagled a deal somehow. He seemed to be very proficient at doing this. So maybe he was headed to Indio (where I discovered later, one of the real estate agents had relocated. Maybe this was a connection?) But more likely to San Diego. I would file this information away and check it out later. Then I called Clarence. I asked him if I could come up and see him. He gave me directions to where he lived at the Desert Hideaway.

When I started out for Clarence's place, I noticed that my gas tank was full. Don had filled it before returning it to the parking spot in front of the clinic!

I pulled into the address that Clarence had given me and I saw that Don's small, but neat-looking trailer that he had shown me on that Sunday when he was arranging for the Chinese dinner, was very close to Clarence's. I also saw a woman dressed casually but nicely, crossing the road to come over to my car.

"Are you looking for Don?" she asked me.

"Well, as a matter of fact I am but right now I'm here to see Clarence."

"Yeah, a lot of people are looking for Don."

News sure did travel fast! Then I saw a very old man getting out of his patio chair and coming my way.

"Christina?"

"Yes, Clarence, I'm Christina."

"Come on over here, away from these busybodies up here! They're something else!" He motioned for me to approach the full-sized trailer, which I assumed was his. When it looked like the busybody wasn't going to go away he said, "Better yet, let's go inside." He motioned for me to go up the steps into his trailer.

Clarence told me the story of how Don had purchased the smaller trailer from him a couple of months before, when he first got to the Desert Hideaway, for $1600.00. He gave him one fourth down and was making payments to him. He also fixed it up considerably, as well as those of the neighbors. He had helped Clarence by doing things in his trailer and taking Clarence into town because Clarence wasn't supposed to drive. He was 92 years old. He told me that he knew when Don called me on Sunday because Don had told him that his battery was down on his cell phone and he had to make "the most important phone call of my life."

"I don't know what happened to Don. When he talked about you, it's like he was a changed man. He just sort of went goofy over you."

"Sure, go ahead and blame me, Clarence," I joked.

"No," Clarence said, "he was happy. He told me he felt like he was 19 years old."

I told Clarence, "Yes he said the same thing to me."

Clarence smiled kindly and said, "And that's what he acted like, a kid, a teenager."

I nodded.

"Well, I don't know why these people are so mad at him. He more than earned that money for the Chinese dinner by doing all the work he did for everybody around here. He owed me a little bit of money for some food he had to buy for one of their dinners but I'm not mad at him. He did plenty of things to help me out. He does have a little tape player of mine that I'd like to get back but if I don't that's okay."

"Did he make his payments like he promised to do?"

"Yes, he did. He got a Social Security check every month. I know because we would go into town and I'd see him deposit it or get money from the bank at the supermarket. And he really did a lot to fix up the trailer. It's spotless. Would you like to see it?"

I told him yes and we went outside. We started walking up the path as Clarence pointed to a nearby trailer which was large and very clean looking with green indoor/outdoor carpet laid on the dirt in the front yard.

"Don did that for them. They're the Chinese Dinner people. He did a lot of other stuff for them too and never got paid a dime. Nothin'. They treated him like dirt. Accused him of stealing."

We went on up to Don's trailer. I noticed that the little tent was gone—the one Don said I could sleep in anytime I wanted.

Inside I remarked about what a clean place it was. It was spotless.

"Oh yes! Don was a clean-freak." He pointed out different things that Don had done to improve the place.

"It looks like he intended to stay here," I mused, "and especially if he was paying you."

"Oh, yes, I think he did plan on staying here. Why else would he do all that he did and pay that money?"

"So where do you think Don went? Why do you think he moved on?" I asked.

Clarence shook his head. "I just don't know. I can't figure it out. He seemed happy enough. People liked him. He had the little trailer here. . ." his voice trailed off.

I changed the subject by asking Clarence where he had lived before coming here. He told me Oregon and that he had moved here many years ago. "I've seen all sorts come and go. A lot stay here most of their lives. Then he revealed some stories about his family to me. He asked me some innocuous questions about myself and then he changed the subject back to Don.

"When did you meet Don? Did you know him before?"

"No, I just met him on Valentine's Day when I came to see my friend Sandi and to listen to music. Where was he before he came here?"

"Well, he told me he was over at Winterhaven and he traveled here with a couple who were from Oregon. They took a liking to him and he was up in Oregon at one time so maybe they knew each other up there."

"Did you ever play cards with Don and the others? He told me he was a professional poker player.

Clarence laughed. "Don? Shoot! The others made fun of him, he was so bad. I don't think he ever won a game." Then he shook his head, "No, I don't like cards. Oh, I used to when I was much younger but I don't see so good now that I'm up in years."

I smiled at this kindly old gentleman and thought that he must have really been something in his earlier years. He was still very polite, wise and humorous and a truly gentle man.

"I'd better go Clarence," I said as I stood up and Clarence stood too, although a bit haltingly.

"Well I hope you'll come back and see me, Christina. You'll always be welcome here and I'm glad I had a chance to meet you."

I promised him that I would come back. We shook hands and I gave him a hug and a kiss on his clean-shaven cheek.

Driving back to my home I pondered over all that Clarence had told me.

When I arrived at my house and walked into the bedroom where my answering machine is, I saw that the message light was blinking red.

"Christina, my name is Gerry. I live at the Desert Hideaway and I understand you were trying to find out information about Don. I think we need to talk. It seems he was dating you and me both at the same time. I'd really like to talk to you so please call me." She gave her number.

During our conversation we both discovered many similarities in the stories that Don told, first to her and then to me. She had met him when he first showed up there and had liked him instantly. She felt a lot of the same compassion for him when he told of his deceased wife and pretty much the same scenario that he had told me later, with only a few minor changes. Gerry had felt that they would make a good pair of travelers. He also told her of his Monaco motor home which was being brought to him "any day now," by his sons. He had added, in my version, that he was going to have it set up on "Snob Hill", the area along the fringes of the Desert Hideaway, where the owners of numerous huge motor homes were in residence along with elaborate solar systems, dishes, antennae and attachments to make their lives more enjoyable, while roughing it in the "wilds."

We talked for an hour. Our conversation ended with me agreeing to join her for breakfast on Sunday at the Alibi, the place where Don had met me for breakfast a week before.

At the breakfast there were several individuals who wanted to hear my story, were eager to hear it, in fact. Among them was the Jeep couple that Don had arranged the Chinese dinner with. They remained pretty much aloof from the rest of us sitting at my table. One man came up to me immediately and voiced strong support for Don and all that he had done for various residents of the Desert Hideaway. Some people seemed reluctant to get involved. Perhaps they sensed that I might pursue the topic of Don and in some way disturb their lifestyle by bringing unwanted attention to their home and thereby endanger their freedom.

After my visit at the Desert Hideaway I was more curious than ever so I went to work following every lead I had. My friend Jane did the same. She had the experience of having worked for a private detective at one time and she knew some creative ways of detecting. I had only the personal contacts I knew Don had made. I started with the bus station.

None of my timelines made sense as far as the bus schedule went so on Monday morning I called the bus station again and talked to a man this time.

"Yes, I remember when he came in, this Peterson guy. The first time he came in he was with a woman, maybe she was that Monica he was supposed to hook up with."

"No, that was me. I came in with him when he checked the bags and bought a ticket."

"Well, then he came in the next day and said that the ticket wasn't going to be used until the following day. I didn't charge him anything for keeping the things in the locker an extra day. It was only a couple of bucks and we weren't busy anyway."

"One thing I can't figure out" I said, "is if the bus left at 10:00 a.m. for San Diego, how could he could have called me at 9:30 and the realtor from the department store at 10:30 or 11?"

The agent looked at me and shook his head. "He didn't go to San Diego."

"But your co-worker told me he had to go to San Diego or Indio. That those were the only destinations that left after 11 o'clock."

"No ma'am. I sold him the ticket. It was to Phoenix. I watched him load his stuff and get on the bus. And it left at 10:00 a.m."

"Well, how could he have called the realtor from that location? She said that's what her caller I.D. said, an 800 number from a department store."

"Because the bus stops on the way to Phoenix. The bus station and the department store share the same parking lot. He had half an hour to make the call and must have used the phone in the store to do it."

I told the ticket agent that we were trying to locate this

guy, along with numerous other people and that maybe this information would be used in a book someday. He seemed pleased with this thought.

So, Don was very adept at covering his tracks. The correct timeline must have been as follows: He left my house at 8:30 a.m., after making several phone calls to real estate agents. Possibly he kept an appointment with the first one that he had spoken to from my house. That was for 9:00 a.m. Then, perhaps, he called others, for I learned that he had spoken to at least two brokers. Jackie's office was in the same block as the first agent's office and that of the clinic. He probably jotted her number down, and went into the clinic where he left my keys He called me at 9:30, to tell me of the change in plans, so that I would prepare for his family's visit. This would keep me busy at my house. Then he continued to the bus station, which was two blocks away. The agent at the station saw him get on the bus headed for Phoenix with all his belongings, shortly before 10:00 a.m. When it made a pit stop. Don went across the parking lot to the department store and called me and, evidently Jackie too, to make an appointment for 2:00 p.m. Sometime in his travels he had stopped at a gas station to fill up my gas tank.

I called several of the phone numbers that Don had jotted down on his list and on my cell phone registry. I had luck with only two agents. Jackie as noted before and another one who told me she had him figured out as a dud from just a few words with him. I remembered this agent from when I was president of the Board of Realtors and having had a slight knowledge of her as an agent. I always thought she acted in a rather flippant manner, sort of a smart aleck.

"What were your first impressions of Don?" I asked Gerry.

"Oh, friendly. Good personality. Intelligent."

Yes, I could see all of those qualities. And more.

Gerry began trying to get some information about Don. She said that the first thing people said to her when she told them why she was calling was, "*Who are you?*"

Here is what she told them,

"My name is Gerry. I'm a retired technical-writer/teacher who travels full-time in my RV. I usually spend my winters at an RV park near Phoenix, a fascinating community of all types of folks, some permanent and some snowbirds.

"Don arrived here in January with a Canadian couple he had befriended while camped at another RV park in Arizona. He had only a tent, claiming that the engine of the van he owned had burned out, so his son arranged to have it and his trailer towed to San Diego for repairs. He soon became the chef for one of the clubs here, made many friends, and told many stories of his life (executive chef for a large hotel chain for 37 yrs.; degree in architecture; doctorate in theology from a Baptist seminary; feeding the hungry throughout the southwest; camp host in Oregon; daughter-in-law Tammy spoon-fed him back to life after he lost the will to live following the death of his wife of 42 yrs.; etc.). In particular, he constantly mentioned his sons, Michael and Kevin, and Tammy. The stories mostly jibed, so few red flags went up.

"He's quite the smooth talker, so shortly after I met him we discussed plans to travel together because we appeared to have the same interests and there appeared to be a mutual attraction. ("Appeared" is the operative word here.) The plans involved borrowing his son's 40+-ft. Monaco motor home and perhaps storing my motor home in his other son's scrap metal yard. Before I took off with him, however, I told him I wanted to verify that he was who he said he was, and that I had found nothing about him on the internet, which is odd. At this time he met a woman who lives in the valley, and began making similar travel plans with her and telling her all the same stories he had told me and others" Seems Don is a chameleon, adapting himself to whoever is his friend of the moment."

"We agree that he's a world-class something, but are not exactly sure what: con man?; pathological liar?; sociopath?; nutcase? We hope you can supply some answers."

His supposedly dead wife responded with this conversation:

"Well, Gerry, I would say you dodged the bullet with this guy! All of what he said was a lie, except I was married to him for 22 years. And, yes he has two sons named Michael and Kevin, both of which want nothing to do with him. I divorced him about 24 years ago, and am happily married. This guy usually went by the name Jack, but has to keep moving because he has many warrants out across many states. He has been in and out of jail for various crimes from theft to kidnapping. He was on Americas Most Wanted a few years back for the kidnapping. I am a Christian and didn't believe in divorce, which he knew when we married. Those were the worst years of my life. Constantly on the move, sometimes leaving in the night, most of the time never knowing what he had done. He is a pathological liar, a compulsive gambler and has an explosive temper. A con man, stealing whatever he can. I'm surprised he is still alive. The last I had heard of him, he was in a stolen U-haul truck in Arizona, jumping probation, kidnapping a teenage girl (who got away) and taking off with $150 stolen money. That was about two years ago. Glad you were smart enough to see through him. So many were not."

I voiced concern about Don's returning to the Valley.

Gerry said, "I don't think we need be concerned. He'll not be back this way any time soon! Too many folks on the lookout for him. How about calling that sheriff you talked to and giving him Don's phone number, along with the background info from his wife They may be searching for him somewhere."

A couple of days later, Gerry said, "Wow! I'm trying to get the other article into a file I can email to people. I'll send you it when I succeed. What are the other articles Jane sent you? Was the deputy going to do anything with his phone number?"

==

I sent this:

"Here's another article. It sounds like the kids weren't in too good shape when Don abducted them. Maybe he was trying to protect them. Maybe that's why he wasn't still in prison.

This article stated the condition of the children that Don abducted, and that it had been too long-standing for it to have been Don's doing."

I sent the article to Gerry and Jane.

Gerry said: "It's unbelievable that he's such a sleaze!!!!! How did we get so snookered?"

Jane said,

"Gross! Christina, you are still trying to give him the benefit of the doubt. He is a transient, lying, embezzling, abusive, thief, convict and lowlife scumbag. You are lucky that that he didn't take advantage of you when you opened up your home and car to him. I just need for you to really come to reality with this. He wasn't romantic as you keep saying because it was all a big joke at your expense. Rick had him pegged immediately and

I wasn't far behind. Until he just disappeared, you told me he was the real deal. That was only hours before he skipped town. I know how trusting you are and that is part of your beautiful charm but I beg you to be more careful and not open your home to anyone until you have completely checked them out.

As a good friend/sister I just had to express my concern. Xoxo"

> I pointed out that, "The article says that they were still trying to determine what he had done. Also that the father of some of the kids was wanted on unrelated drug charges."
>
> Jane said, "Back then he was wanted in FIVE states!!!!"

Gerry had located his cell phone number. She said, "I'm not sure what we should do with this, but here's his number. I'd like to find out what his name really is.

There are many places where you can pay to get the name that goes with the number. This is the cheapest I found. I'm thinking about doing this."

I said, "Why don't I just call the number?"

I called the number and the recorded message that I got said that it hadn't been set up to receive messages.

"Hi Gerry,

"Well, Finally!! After trying every day to get a hold of someone, the original investigating deputy called me back. I had even more info to give him after Jane learned that Don Peterson had been wanted in five states. She sent me links to some articles and one of them said he was on America's Most Wanted list. I can send you links to those sites. The deputy listened to me but he said that there wasn't anything he could do, really. He had checked him out locally and found nothing. He congratulated me and my friends on our 'great detective work.' "

Nearly one year later

In response to my search for facts I had this conversation with Don's ex-wife's husband:

"Yes, he had psychiatric treatment while in jail in Arizona and was on medication. but he made a deal with someone to open a camp and then ran off. He has been wanted by the Hell's Angels amongst others. He is a top notch con man and duped his wife into marrying him. That turned into a nightmare for her and she stayed with him for years as he threatened to kill her sons if she left. It was very traumatizing for her. He was on America's Most Wanted and was sentenced to prison in Idaho but somehow got out of it. You are lucky if he didn't take you for all you had. He has worked as a short order cook and a scrapper."

I told him some of the stories Don had told us.

"That's pretty funny. His ex wife is alive and well after divorcing him in 1990. His daughter in law at the time never met him or wanted to after what he did to his sons. He has no house in San Diego (lives off of conning others) and has never owned one out right due to paranoia issues of the law. He has two sons; one that has just graduated from college as a Psychologist (lives in LA) and the other is in the Air force (been in the air force for 16 years) lives in Sacramento. Neither one will have anything to do with him and one son, to protect his mother had Don arrested in Reno. He has no family members living in San Diego and I understand his own sister is afraid of him and won't give out her address to anyone. And on it goes. He is his own worst enemy and in my belief, delusional.

He always manages a little truth with the lies so that is

what makes it easy to believe. Glad no one was hurt by his antics in the valley."

And so . . .

I will always wonder who was on the other end of the line when he made many, many calls. Maybe there was no one. I wonder if his trip to Phoenix was a planned one or a spur of the moment. It was February when he headed out, a beautiful time of year. I will wonder if he will move on to a cooler climate when the desert turns excruciatingly hot.

I am of the opinion that some of the stories told by others may be slightly exaggerated. Don showed no evidence of having a fiery temper. If he had been guilty of kidnapping, why weren't charges pressed against him? What caused the bedsores on the child's head sitting in his car seat that were reported in the newspaper? Scabs don't form in that short period of time. It didn't happen in two days. He had to have been neglected for a much longer time.

If Don had a history of theft and warrants against him for the same, why did he not steal from me, Clarence, Gerry—people who trusted him and afforded him the opportunity to do so? Why did he feel it necessary to refill my gas tank?

Was he hesitant to drive my car because he held no driver's license? He did have a bank account, according to Clarence, and had his Social Security checks deposited into it.

Why did he do so many things such as repairs, improvements for so many without repayment?

He was scrupulously clean about himself and his living quarters.

How did he have that great amount of knowledge about such a wide variety of things?

So many questions. So few answers.

16

A MOST PERSISTENT STALKER

David

This man was a fine, upstanding citizen of our local community. His family was well-respected, and seemingly at first, so was he. All of them were regular church-goers.

I felt sorry for him after listening to his tales of medical problems and grew to like some of the conversations we had about various subjects. Then he became increasingly demanding of my time and attention. He telephoned me constantly. He followed me. He left messages at my house on the patio when I wouldn't answer his phone calls. He showed up in places he knew I frequented. He stalked me.

I met David at a social club where I was a new member. I was there for Taco Tuesday, and afterwards I sat at the bar talking with John. John looked like Roy Orbison and was an excellent dancer—jitterbug. When we danced we got a standing ovation from everyone including the band, if there was one.

Everyone seemed to know David when he walked into the club that night, hugging him, patting him on the back, etc. He sat at the end of the bar and called over to John, asking who the gorgeous creature sitting beside him was. John ignored him and we went on with our conversation. Then David got up, walked over to us and asked him again, rather insistently. John introduced us. Subsequently, I had some conversation with David and told him I didn't usually go to that club, that I belonged to another club in a nearby town and that I had first joined there because they had karaoke on Friday nights.

David said "You weren't there last Friday night." I told him no, I didn't like to go in there much because of all the gossip and high drama in the place. We talked some more, while John looked on with evident disgust. Then David wrote his phone number on a napkin and asked me to call him sometime, the sooner the better. He said he enjoyed talking to me.

I called him the next morning.

4/27-Wed

I gave David directions and he came to my house. He said he was interested in hearing more about the books I'm writing. I read him a few things. We enjoyed talking, about politics mostly, because that seemed to be the subject that he felt pretty excited about. We had the same political leanings. He told me about his family, long time residents of our valley and well-known. and respected. His grandfather had been a judge. He told me about his numerous health issues and felt he had been a miracle because the doctors had given him 48 hours to live and sent him home to die. He's had Hepatitis C and his liver had shut down. Then he was put on a very expensive drug treatment, $200,000, and cured. The doctors said it was a miracle. He also still had diabetes but he doesn't believe in medication and he knew how to control it. After a couple of hours, we decided to go to grab a bite of lunch. My daughter had given me a gift card. David said he had one too, so I thought maybe he was accustomed to going there. I was not. We used my $20 card for our sandwiches. We talked for a couple of hours then I drove back to my house in my Jaguar which I had decided to drive over. David stayed for a while talking and then asked me if I wanted to go out.

We went to the lodge. I drove my car and David drove his Mercedes SUV. We played pool, listened to music, had a couple of drinks and stayed until they were ready to close at 8:30. Then David suggested another place where they had music and pool tables. I drove. We had two drinks, played three games of pool, had some nachos and left. I took David back to get his car.

He kissed me a few times, tried to get friendlier and I told him I was leaving. He asked me if he could come over to my house. I said no. Driving home I noticed his SUV following behind me on the highway but staying at a distance. When I got to the turn to go home, I noticed he turned behind me so I sped up a couple of blocks, made a few quick turns to lose him and then I didn't see his SUV behind me any longer so I went on home. Shortly after I got there David called me.

He said "What were you doing? It looked like you didn't want me to go to your house."

I told him that that's what I had said.

He said "No, you told me I could come over."

I told him he was mistaken. I had never told him that nor would I have done that. I told him he thought heard what he wanted to hear.

4/28- Thurs.- David called —I told him I was busy doing things around the house.

SOMEONE IS WATCHING... AND WAITING.

4/29- Fri.-

David invited me to a birthday party for his nephew. I was to meet his sister (that he lived with) and nieces and nephews. His family were all well known, well off and very respectable. And religious. And none of them drank. When we got to the restaurant we were too early, so David suggested we go to another restaurant that had liquor, for a drink. Then David drove to the party. He cautioned me to not say anything about our having a drink.

The dinner was very nice. His family which consisted of brothers, sisters, in-laws, nieces and nephews and grandkids, were all friendly. I was surprised when he told his family about the incident of me trying to lose him when we left The Moose. He smiled strangely when he told this story. I didn't know if he was trying to impress them with my reluctant actions, or what.

After dinner David and I went to the Moose, where they were having a private remembrance party for one of the member's sons who had died several years before. David was driving. When we came back to my house he had another drink and I noticed that he was nodding off. Then he fell to the floor and looked like he was trying to stay awake. I asked him if he was okay and he said he would be okay. He could drive. I told him no, he might kill somebody. He was unable to drive so he'd have to stay at my house. I had told him I didn't like men staying at my house because I didn't want to be the topic of gossip for my neighbors or to worry my daughter who lived next door. But I didn't think it was a good idea for him to be driving in that condition.

I showed him the guest room and the bathroom and laid out a towel and washcloth for him. He said he had to make a trip to his car. When he came back we said goodnight. He went into the guest room and I went into my bedroom at the other end of the house. I locked the door behind me.

The next morning a strange noise woke me. I got up and went from my bedroom to go see what it was. The door to the spare room was open, I saw that David wasn't there. I went out to the kitchen and on into the laundry room. The back door was wide open. I always keep it double-locked. I looked in my driveway and saw that David's SUV was gone. When he called me later he said that he'd gone to get some coffee and he was waiting for it to get a little later so he could go home. I told him to come over later and I'd make breakfast. After that we could go to the club.

4/30, Saturday

We went to the club, played pool and played the jukebox. David interrupted a game of pool he was playing with one of the men and came up to me several times at the jukebox and then he said, "All those guys are hitting on you. They all want you."

I shrugged it off. When we left around 6:00 p.m. so I could go feed my daughter's dogs, a couple of the guys were standing outside, smoking.

One of the men said, "Why don't you take that guy home and come back over and see me?"

The other man said, "No, get rid of him and come back and see ME!"

Driving home I told David I thought they were crude and rude. I went by a fast-food place and got two egg burritos for our supper, which I took home. Then I went over to feed the dogs. When I came home, we ate our burritos and then David started falling asleep in the middle of our conversation so I told him he needed to go home. I didn't feel this was dangerous since he hadn't been drinking. He wanted to stay and I told him no.

5/1 Sunday

David called and wanted me to go somewhere. I told him I didn't want to go. Later in the afternoon he called again and said, What are you doing?" I told him nothing, just playing on the computer.

"Why don't you come over to the club? John's with me and they won't let us in without you."

I told him to just ring the buzzer.

He said, "John and I are here and we'll just drive around and wait if you'll come over."

I repeated to ring the buzzer.

Then, after much wheedling from David, I said okay, maybe I'd go and have a drink. When I got there John and David were in the club already having a beer. We listened to music on the jukebox. I danced the fast ones with Don and the slow ones with David. I went home. After taking John home David called me and wanted to come over. I told him no.

5/2 Monday

I agreed to go to the club with David. From there we went to another club in separate cars and played pool. Both of us left early. David knew I was leaving on Wednesday to go to San Diego to meet my friend Sharon. He called me the next day, Tuesday.

5/3 Tuesday

6:00 a.m. David called and said he was sitting outside my house. He was trying to get information on low-cost housing so he could move out of his sister's house. I told him to go to his club because they had the number of their sponsored low-income housing. I told him I had to pack and get ready for my trip the next day.

5/4 Wednesday

David called early in the morning and wondered if I'd help him and get some numbers for him so he could find out about the housing. He said the lady at his club had given him a wrong number. I got busy calling the housing authority, who gave me some numbers for David to call. David wanted to come over because he wasn't going to see me for a few days. I told him no. I had to get on the road.

At 2:30 I was in the timeshare elevator in San Diego, trying to load the luggage cart to take up to my room when my cell phone started ringing. I wedged the door open and answered. It was David.

"I called those numbers and nobody will call me back!"

"David, I can't talk to you now. I'm trying to get in the elevator. . . . I'll call you later."

When I called later, I got his voice mail. I left a message asking if he'd had any luck. I didn't hear from him that night, Wednesday, or until 10:30 Thursday night.

5/5 Thursday, 10:30 p m. My cell phone rang.

"Whatcha doin'?"

"I'm sitting with my friends, talking."

"Well, I'm at the club and I'm hearing a bunch of stuff and I don't know what to believe."

"What are you hearing?"

"Well, things about you and I don't know what's true."

"Like what?"

"Oh, where should I begin?" He sighed, sounding very dramatic.

I was getting mad by this time. "Begin with what you heard. Spit it out! Those people don't know anything about me!"

"No, I don't want to say anything, I probably said too much already. But I don't want to stand in your way, if you've got plans that don't include me. I just want you to be happy."

"Well, if you won't tell me what's bothering you, hang up! Goodbye!"

My friends in the condo heard my side of the conversation but they said nothing. The next morning as Sharon was cooking breakfast for us, she asked me what was going on.

I gave a short account of what David had been doing.

She shook her head and said, "Dump him! You don't need that in your life."

5/7 Saturday

My friends and I went to Old Town for the Cinco de Mayo celebration. I left San Diego and arrived at my house at 3:00 p.m. I had wanted to get home early enough to go to a rib cook-off event that they were having but I was too late. I watched the Kentucky Derby at my house, fed my daughter's pets next door and went to the club. As soon as I went in I saw that it was crowded and there was no place at the bar for me to sit. My friend Carmen grabbed a barstool and brought it over and wedged it between her and Karen. I asked Karen what was happening.

"What do you mean?"

"Oh, what's happening? What's been going on?"

Well, your friend has been mouthing off and causing trouble."

"Who?"

I thought she meant John, who she had had a contentious history with but she pointed over to the bar and said, "Your friend there, what's his name?"

I looked to see who she meant and saw David sitting over to the side.

"David?"

"Yeah, he's been shooting his mouth off. He told me on Thursday that he had something to tell me and then he said he'd better not say anything. He'd probably said too much already."

I told her that was practically the same words he had used when he called me in San Diego at 10:30 Thursday night. He said that he'd been hearing things about me. But he wouldn't tell me what and he'd "probably said too much already."

Then I noticed David getting up and walking outside. I said I wondered where he was going.

Karen said, "Probably outside to smoke."

I said, "But he doesn't smoke."

She looked at me. "Oh, yes he does."

"He told me he doesn't and one time I thought I smelled smoke on him and asked him if someone who smoked had been in his car and if that's why he smelled faintly of smoke. He said he didn't smoke."

Karen called the barmaid over and asked her if David smoked when he went outside to talk with them and use his cell phone.

She said, "He sure does!"

5/8 Mother's Day

I went to the free breakfast with Katy at a club in a nearby town. David called me later that morning and left a message and asked if he could take me for a ride to the mountains. I decided to go to another social club by myself. While sitting there I checked my phone and there were a couple of messages, Mother's Day wishes, and missed calls on my home phone and cell phone. One of them was David asking me why I wouldn't at least talk to him. I was sitting listening to music when my cell phone rang. I told him I didn't want to speak to him and to quit calling me. He said he just didn't understand. Why didn't I want to talk to him. What had he done?

I told him he was a liar and I hung up. About half an hour later I was standing at the jukebox and felt someone touch my arm. It was David.

"I was hoping we could go get dinner or go to the mountains."

"I'm not going anywhere with you!" I went back and sat at the bar.

David went to the opposite side of the bar and sat for about 20 minutes, then he left. I waited for about five minutes more and then I left too, telling one of the men at the bar that I wanted to make sure that my Jaguar wasn't getting scratched up in the parking lot.

Later that afternoon, David called me. He wanted to know if I would go with him to his niece's house, they were going to play some games.

"Inside games or outside games?" I wanted to know.

"Oh they play Dominoes, Clue, that type of thing."

That sounded innocent enough and I already knew that no one in his family drank, so I said okay, I would pick him up. He gave me directions to his sister's house. I figured this would give me a chance to find out what he was talking about and what he was lying about.

On the drive over I mentioned about what Karen had told me and David said "Why do you believe these people and not me? I just wanted to talk to her but she told me to leave her alone."

"Well why would she say you said almost the exact words you said to me about 'having something to say but you'd better not, you'd said too much already'?"

He didn't know. He said, "I've never lied to you and I never will. I hate a liar!"

We played games for about two hours and then I took him home early and told him I would be studying hard in the next few days for my upcoming driver's test.

5/9 Monday.

I was studying, determined to pass the test. I was worried about it because of my upcoming trip to Kansas in four weeks. I had a lot of driving ahead of me and couldn't afford to be without a license. David called me and wanted to know if I wanted to go out.

"I told you I'm going to be studying all day."

"I just thought you might need a break."

"No, I don't!" I hung up.

Later, David called again, "Still studying?"

"Yes!"

"I don't know what you're worried about. You're smart, you'll pass."

"David, quit calling me!" I hung up.

5/10 Tuesday

Next morning, more of the same.

"I thought I could take you out to get something to eat."

"NO!"

"Maybe I could bring something over to you?"

"NO! Quit bugging me!"

5/11, Wednesday

I passed my test. But I wasn't feeling well. I called David that evening as I had promised I would, to tell him I had passed,

"Good, do you want to have a drink?"

"No David, I'm sick to my stomach. I don't want anything."

I heard some noise in the background and I asked him where he was.

"Outside my house. There's an airport here, that's what you heard."

About half an hour later John called, asking me how I was doing. He said that David had told him I was sick.

"Where was he when he told you?"

"At the club, about half an hour ago. Then I came over here to the restaurant and called you. Yeah, he was outside the club talking to you on the phone and then he came in and told me you were sick."

"Well he told me he was outside his house and why did he think he had to report to you anyway? And then lie to me about it?"

The next time David called I told him I didn't want to talk to him ever again.

5/12 Thursday —I went to a restaurant and danced with John. Girls took photos. One invited us to go to a birthday party on Saturday.

5/13—stayed home

5/14—

I picked John up, went to the party, left about 10, went for a drink after, took John home and I came home.

5/15 stayed home

5/16 stayed home

5/17—

About 11:00 am there was knocking on my kitchen door. I looked out the front window and saw David's SUV. I turned the TV off and went to look out the window, just as he was closing the patio gate. Then he knocked at the front door. I picked up my phone, dialed his number, got the machine and told him I was going to call the police. I told him he wasn't welcome at my house and he'd better leave. Then I heard knocking at the back door again and then again at the front. I was really frightened. This neighborhood is pretty much deserted in the morning. When I saw him drive off I waited a little bit and then went out and found a note on the bench.:

"Hi Marry (sic), Came by to see you. Why don't you call me. OK!!! David"

I called my friend Katy.

She said, "He sounds like a nut."

I asked her if she'd go with me to Taco Tuesday because I didn't want to go alone. We went. As soon as I got there the bartender told me that David had been in there drinking since early afternoon. When he came in, the back of his head was bloody. He'd fallen down. He said David had told him that John had screwed him over with me and caused us to break up.

Then John came in to the club and I told him and Katy what the bartender had said. Katy urged me to call David. I didn't want to, but she said it was only right that I should check on him, since he had been a friend of mine. I felt guilty so I called, got his machine and said that I had heard that he had blood on him and I was concerned about that.

John seemed upset that I would call him, saying something like, "She's back with him again." Then he stormed off.

All of these childish theatrics were really beginning to annoy me.

Katy and I went into the dining hall to eat. When we came out to the bar our barstools were occupied so we had to sit over by the pool table. I went up to John and asked him why he hadn't saved our place. He said he had just come over to talk to another friend. I noticed David was now sitting two barstools over. I went over to him and asked him what had happened. He said he thought his sugar level was bad. I told him he needed to take care of that and go see a doctor.

I went back and sat with Katy.

David got into a lengthy discussion with John after that and soon John left, without telling me goodbye. He had given me a little stuffed mouse that he'd gotten out of the vending machine. Katy commented that that was strange that he hadn't even said goodbye. Then we left, with Maria telling us to watch, that there was a lot of lightning and it was raining. Katy said David just sat there with this silly big smile on his face. I asked her if he looked threatening.

"No, just like he was happy to see you."

5/19 Thursday

I went out on my patio and saw a note on the orange bench, written on the back of a prescription from for diabetes testing. It read:

"I went to Dr and was locked out Don't have my phone or any of my things. So I don't know what I am going to do! Can't test my suger (sic)and am sure it's bad Can't write very good. Aerything(sp) has been 'moderated'? (won't let me put how he spelled the word) mode …rted(sp), By family and face book and don't know the rest. Help me! David"

I thought the note was put there the night before (Wednesday) because when I was standing in the kitchen I saw that my patio motion sensor light went on to bright and I wondered what had set it off.

Saturday and still no word from David. I thought he might be lurking around. I thought he might be in the hospital. I thought he might be dead. I called his sister's number. She said that he had cracked his head on her coffee table and was in the hospital, in a coma. He had pneumonia and some other infection. He was in bad shape. She said his sugar was okay and it wasn't caused by alcohol. The doctors were still doing tests. I felt somewhat relieved that he wasn't stalking me and somewhat guilty that I had talked so mean to him. But I kept telling myself that he just would not listen to me. I played his constant messages which I had saved on my cell phone and house phone. So insistent, so garbled and confused and confusing.

David was in the hospital with double pneumonia. His sister told me in the first account that he was in a coma and in really bad shape. The second account said that he wasn't much improved. Third: he showed slight improvement and was trying to speak but they couldn't understand him. He was responding to verbal commands.

I went in to have a tooth pulled and didn't check on him for a couple of days. When I called the hospital one week after he'd been taken to the hospital. I was told that they were releasing him. I called his cell phone four days later and he answered, sounding very weak and groggy and said that he was in the hospital in San Diego in rehab. I called two days later and he sounded much better. He said it was a senior assisted-living place and that his sister in San Diego had gotten him in there. He would be evaluated on Friday and then go to live with his son in the Sacramento area to get himself straight.

David left the Valley but he was still stalking me long distance two months later. I was on vacation in Pittsburgh and I checked my cell phone and saw messages. I listened to them and it was David with his same old garbled dialogue: "Why don't you talk to me?" "I wish you would call me." "Call me!" Then I checked my house phone in California and heard the messages that he had left on the machine. Same thing.

I returned home in August.

I hope when cooler weather comes to the Valley it doesn't bring David with it.

2/14/17—six months later.

David's back in town. I saw him at the club tonight. The bartender said that he was in yesterday—three times and again today—three times. John, my friend from before, who David was trying to cause trouble for, told me David was back in town. While I was sitting there David came in again. He stayed at the other end of the bar. He didn't try to talk to me.

I played the jukebox and when John came over and asked me to dance, David left.

I wonder if that was David who came into my yard yesterday? Driving a small, very dark grey car? It wasn't his tan Mercedes SUV that he was driving last year. Nobody could tell me what he's driving now.

Wednesday

I went to have my mammogram done. Afterwards I stopped in the club and asked the bartender if he would do me a favor and if David came in would he check to see what car he was driving. He said she would and I should call him later.

I called him back at 2:00 p.m.

"Did David come in?"

"Yep."

"Did you see the car he was driving?"

"Sure did. A dark grey, almost black sedan."

"So it was David that came to my house."

"I got the license number. Do you want it?"

"Yes!" I grabbed a pen.

I asked him if David said anything when he came in. He said, "No, he just sat there. Besides I don't talk to him—I don't like him."

I ran a quick check on the license plate and it said Toyota Corolla, 2016. I couldn't imagine that David would be able to afford that car, considering what he had indicated his finances were like only a few months before and that he was going to have to look for subsidized housing. I thought he was probably driving a rental or that he had borrowed it from someone.

Sunday I went to the club. Angela came up to me and said

she'd had a dream about, "That guy that you danced with—that little guy."

"David?"

"Yes, that guy. I had a dream about him and he looked awful. He had cancer or something."

"When did you have the dream?"

"A couple of nights ago."

I told her, "David's been stalking me."

Angela's eyes widened.

Minutes later I was in the ladies' room when Angela came rushing in.

"He's here!"

"Who, David?"

"Yes and he looks awful, like he's been in a fight or something."

She opened the door and whispered, "I'll go out this side exit so he won't see that I came in to tell you."

I went out to the bar and sat in my usual spot at the end of the bar so I could see everything that was going on. I glanced over and David did look awful, not beaten up but haggard. He probably is sick. Maybe it's cancer. Or maybe he did get beaten up since I saw him on Tuesday night. Maybe John beat him up.

Another member told me a week later that David had told him that he had spent a week at my house. He told him, "It was like heaven."

I decided to tell as many people as I could about David's stalking and that he was living in a fantasy world. I also let my neighbors know. I told my friend, the police chief. I also told him that I had saved many of the recorded messages from David and the notes that he left on my patio bench, imploring me to talk to him. The chief jotted down his private telephone and cell phone numbers for me to use to "get quick help."

Then I went on my summer trips for June and July. I

returned to the valley in August. When football season began I watched the games at one of the social clubs. I also stopped in the club in the adjacent town and watched some of the games there.

Nobody has seen David for four weeks. I can only hope that he's disappeared from my life forever, for good this time.

One month later:

Yesterday when I went to the club David was sitting in a barstool next to John, a friend of mine, who was the same person that David had accused of "breaking us up". I thought they were talking about me when I noticed John say something surreptitiously to David and nudge him when he saw me walk in.

I proceeded past them and the stalker said, "Hey! HEY!" I didn't respond.

David said, "You don't know who I am."

I said coldly, "I know who you are."

I continued to walk past them. There were four men, friends of mine who knew my history with the stalker, sitting at another table. One of them, Larry, said, "Come here, sit with us, we'll protect you." He asked me what I would like to drink and went to get it at the bar. After a few minutes I got up from the table to borrow a pen from the bartender.

David, the stalker came up to me and asked, "Why are you acting so cranky?"

"I'm not cranky."

"Well, why won't you talk to me?"

"I don't want to talk to you!"

"I can see that but why? Why don't you want to talk to me?"

"Because I don't like you!"

The barmaid heard this conversation.

I asked John a few days later what they were talking about. He confirmed my suspicions that David was talking about me and John's telling him to shush, I had just walked in. Then he said that David had been telling him again about all the time he spent with me in my house and it was heaven. John said David was asking him about what had gone on between him and me. John told him, "nothing." David asked him if he'd ever been to my house. John told him no, that he didn't even know where I lived.

It worried me that someone might believe David. I told John if David and I had been so "heavenly" together, you would think I would have some memory of that and furthermore, why then would I find him so loathsome and want nothing to do with him? Why would he have left messages on the bench on my patio, imploring me to talk to him? Why the numerous messages on my cell phone and house phone begging me to talk to him? Why would I find him despicable and not want to speak to him or have anything to do with him?

A week later another admirer of mine confided in me that David had regaled him with stories of spending many days and nights with me. On one of these "dates" we supposedly had gone to a popular motel/restaurant, where they had a secret room in the back where orgies and nudity were a regular occurrence and that David and I had indulged in both. Also in his tall tales were the stories about things (not named) that I did to David and his tickling me and making me giggle. I don't giggle.

I'm sure the restaurant would like to know about this den of iniquity. Actually we did go to this place on our first date, as stated in the beginning of this story. There were several pool tables and a jukebox in a back room off the lounge. I had been in this lounge a couple of years before when they had karaoke, but it was a younger crowd, singing mostly Mexican songs so I never went back.

This night David and I played pool. We played music. We had some nachos and a couple of drinks. Then I took David back to the Moose where he had left his SUV. He kissed me aggressively and asked me if he could come to my house. I told him no.

He said, "You know you want me to."

I said, "No, I don't want you to! Good night."

I left the parking lot and soon I saw his car in the rear view mirror. He was following me. So I made some quick turns away from my usual route home. Then I sped up a side street, made a couple more turns, and went on home. There was no Mercedes SUV behind me.

I pulled the car into my garage and quickly pressed the button to close the overhead door. Once inside my house I began to change my clothes. The phone rang. It was David.

"Hey, what were you doing? It looked like you were trying to lose me."

"I was!"

"Well, why? You said you wanted me to go to your house."

"No, I did not. I told you clearly that I didn't want you to come over."

David was and is living in a dream world. He was and is greatly affected by his mixture of medicine and liquor.

I will stop going to places I think he might frequent. Maybe this will be the end of the persistent stalker.

No, that was not to be. Two days ago I went to the club. I wanted to see some of my friends that I hadn't seen for about two months, since I had been out of town. I wasn't there very long, talking about the Super Bowl with some of the fellows that had been following football with me before I went on my trip, when David walked in. He saw me sitting there. I froze when I saw him.

"Hey Girl, whatcha been doing?"

I ignored him. He walked on and sat down by another friend of mine. I heard David say that he had just been at our Mid-winter fair. This is at a fairgrounds very close to my house which is about ten miles from the club. He looked over at me a number of times. The longer I sat there the more irritated I grew, to think that he thought he could get away with telling all his lies about me. The people he was telling didn't know much about me but they had known David for a long period of time and for all I knew, they might believe his lies. I decided to confront him. I walked over to where he sat.

"Why are you telling people lies about you and me?" I demanded to know.

"What? I'm not telling anything about you! What was I supposed to have said?"

"That you and I went to a nude orgy in the backroom of a restaurant."

"That's ridiculous! I don't even know where that is!"

"Yes, you do. You and I went there on our first date. We played three games of pool, listened to music and had nachos. Then I took you back to your car. You tried to follow me home but I ditched you."

"Well. I didn't say anything."

I walked away. A little later I went to the jukebox and was playing some songs when David came up to me.

"I never said anything like that. Just who was I supposed to be saying these things to?"

I told him the name of the man who had told me about the restaurant orgy incident.

"That's nuts! I don't even know him!"

"Oh, you do too. You talk to him all the time."

"And you were mouthing off to John, asking him if he'd ever been to my house."

David went back and sat down but pretty soon he came back to the jukebox. He grabbed my arm.

"C'mon, let's dance."

"I'm not dancing with you!" I flung his hand off and walked away.

David followed me and said, "I know where John lives. Come on, let's go there and we'll see about this!"

"I'M NOT GOING ANYWHERE WITH YOU!"

He walked away, yelling, "They're all a bunch of f - - - - - - liars!! And if you believe them, you're an f - - - - - - fool!"

I yelled, "SHUT UP!!"

The barmaid came over to me. "Are you okay?"

"Yes. I'm okay."

"What was that all about? I saw him go over to you and then I heard him. He sounds like a nut!"

"He's a stalker. Some of the guys in here know about our history."

"I couldn't believe it when he started cussing you."

Then David left. I took my cell phone out of my purse and pulled up the photos that I had taken of the notes David left on my patio. I had taken these shots to show my friend, the chief of police. Now I showed them to the barmaid. She scrutinized them. It is pretty hard to make out exactly what he is saying because he seems agitated, desperate and has many misspellings.

After spending some time on the notes, the barmaid shook her head and said, "Weird!"

Then I noticed the men coming in from the back entrance. One of them came over to me and said, "Don't worry. He's not going to bother you. We're not going to stand for that."

Two nights later I went to the club for Taco Tuesday. I went alone. I went early, thinking that I might avoid David if he should come in. I was waiting for the kitchen to open up to take orders when John walked in. He looked over at me and had a sheepish look on his face. Then David walked in, looking violent. I picked up my drink and glass of water and walked into the dining room.

When I was finished, after eating one of the tacos, I packed up the rest of the dinner and asked Larry if I could go out the back way. He said sure and showed me the gate that took me around to where my car was parked, down just a few parking spaces from the main entrance. David was standing outside the door, smoking. I hurried and opened the car and sped off. I don't know if David saw me or not.

St. Patrick's Day was approaching. I wanted to go out and my place of preference would have been the club where I was now afraid to go. I was afraid to go to any of my usual places for fear David would be looking for a fight. I stayed home. The next day, Sunday, I went to the club in the afternoon. I hadn't seen one of my good friends for three months. She had taken a cruise in that time and I wanted to see how she liked it.

As soon as I walked in Angela came rushing up and asked, "Did you hear what happened to David?"

"No, what?"

"He was in here last night and he was drinking and he fell and hit his head! The police came and the paramedics. Even the fire department! He looked bad, really bad!"

Just then Larry approached me and said, "I see you've heard about David."

"Yes, where is he?"

"I dunno. The cops took him away in an ambulance. He came in. He'd been drinking before he got here. Then he started causing trouble. We refused to serve him any more. We asked him to leave. He went out and before you know it someone rushed in and said David fell and was all bloody. We dialed 911. His car's still out there."

Then Angela was talking to some of the others in the bar. She sounded worried. I told her she should call the hospital to see how he was. She did and shook her head while she was hearing what they said.

"He's not there!"

"Then call the police, they should know where he is."

She called the police. They told her they didn't know where he was. Then Angela began to worry that he might be lying in a ditch somewhere.

One of the men said, "Here's his cell phone. He just left it."

I looked at it and told Angela she needed to call one of his family members. Somebody had to know why he wasn't in the local hospital where the ambulance took him.

She dialed one of the numbers and got a message machine. She was reluctant to leave a message so she dialed another number. This turned out to be a brother in Arkansas. He had no knowledge of his brother's accident or his whereabouts. Angela told him the story and he said he was going to call David's sister or his niece where he was now living.

Several phone calls turned up the news that David had cut his head severely and might be bleeding in his brain. Also the sister said that he had a bad liver and wasn't supposed to be drinking. This had been true also two years before. She said he had been flown to San Diego to a hospital there.

David's car had been sitting unlocked in the parking lot all of Saturday night and half of the next day. I told Angela to come with me and we would get all the contents out of his car and store them in the club. We put everything from the glove box in one plastic bag and everything else in another big plastic bag and gave the bags to the commander. He stored them in a corner of the club.

I would go the next day and see what the news is.

I'm glad I stayed home that night. I'm certain David would have been looking for me and we would have had a confrontation when he found me.

I slept a little better that night, knowing that David was sleeping in a hospital bed.

Two days later I was at the club for Taco Tuesday. I figured David would be in the hospital for several days and it was safe for me to go there. But Angela told me he was going to be released that day. She wondered how he was going to get down to the valley to get his car and phone. She knew that a bus went by close to the hospital in San Diego and made stops nearby the club. She supposed that that was how he would travel.

I was sitting at a table with the man who had told me about the nightclub gossip. I told him what the latest was with David and how he denied even knowing him and said he certainly never said any such thing as what I had been told. The man was silent for a while. Then he said that when David asked about me recently he told him that I sold my house and moved away. Apparently this man likes to make up stories too.

"Yes, David was asking about you a few weeks ago, if I'd seen you and I said no, not for a few months. Then I said that you must have sold your house and moved away."

After dinner I went back into the bar and was sitting, talking with Angela and a few of my men friends. I danced with two of them. Angela said that David's sister and her husband had come in to get his things. I hadn't seen them. Then David walked in.

He walked past me without saying anything and on down

to the end of the bar. A look of surprise was on a few of the people's faces; the barmaid who had heard his cussing me out, my friends who knew our history, Angela. I watched him order three drinks and down them very quickly. Then he left.

I moved over to one of the high tables where three of my big, husky, male friends were sitting. I danced with two of them. Then David walked in and went back to where he had been sitting before. He ordered another drink. It looked like vodka tonic. Angela came over and said she was going to call David's sister and tell her that David was getting drunk again. She went outside. When she came back in I asked her what his sister had said.

"She said, 'You can lead a horse to water but you can't make it drink.'"

Somebody needed to stop him. It doesn't bother me that he's killing himself or may have an accident and do it faster than his bad liver will, but my concern is that he might kill someone else while he's driving around drunk.

Three days later I had to go to the club because I had volunteered to serve desserts for a fundraiser. I planned to leave early, by the side door. I wanted no more confrontations with David, even if it meant that I had to find a safer place to spend my time.

I stayed away for two weeks. Then I started to feel bad that I hadn't seen some of my good friends, so I decided after having breakfast I would go over to the club. If I drove into the parking lot and saw David's SUV I wouldn't stop. Or if I didn't see it and went into the club and David came in, I would leave immediately.

I said hello to some people and went up to two friends and hugged them. Maria said, "Christina, I haven't seen you in so long. Where have you been?"

"I don't feel safe coming in here now."

She sort of nodded her head.

Then the two women were sort of huddled together talking and Arlene said, "Christina will you come outside? I want to talk to you."

"Have you heard the latest, about David?"

"You mean about him falling and cutting his head?"

"No, it's something else. He was in an accident. Another one."

I had been afraid of this.

"Was anybody else hurt? Was David hurt?"

"He's dead."

Then she gave me some of the details and fortunately that no one else was hurt.

Maria told me later that she thought David just didn't want to live anymore. She repeated this the next time I saw her. I didn't ask her why she thought this.

Later I was telling a friend about his death and I said I felt guilty because I felt a rush of relief when I heard that he was gone. He told me not to feel guilty, that it was natural for me to feel that way.

Details of the accident are as follows:

David was driving at a high rate of speed, heading north (probably to the club) It was Taco Tuesday and around 6:00 p.m. He hit two vehicles traveling north also. His SUV began swerving. He continued on and hit another vehicle which was stopped at the traffic light by the shopping center. His SUV flipped over, trapping him under it. He was air-lifted to San Diego. The newspaper article said he was drunk. It said that the police wanted to talk to any witnesses or anyone who might have information. It also said that the other people had minor injuries.

I wondered where he had been drinking? Somewhere close

to my house? Was he hurrying to get to the club for Taco Tuesday because he thought I might be there?

I looked for more facts and learned that he had died two days after the accident. His services at the mortuary will be next Wednesday. I won't go. Two years of stalking is over.

Incidental Pursuits, 17,18,19,20,21

The Sailor

I was twelve years old and in the seventh grade. I met Chickie who was three years older than I was.

One night Chickie and I went on a double date with two sailors. My date was Jim After parking the car and drinking a little bit of beer, which I had a taste of and decided I didn't like it, Chickie and her date got out of the car, to pursue I knew not what. Jim proceeded to force himself on me. I extricated myself out of his groping and grasping hands and told him I wanted to get out of the car.

He then said, derisively, "You know what they're doing out there, don't you?" He was referring to his sailor buddy and Chickie.

"I don't care what they're doing! I'm not going to!"

"How old are you anyway?" Jim snarled.

"Sixteen," I lied.

I guess he decided I was still jailbait because he let me out of the car. I fully intended to walk back to town, which as it turned out would have been about five miles along a lonely highway. I didn't even know for sure where I was but I was determined not to let Jim have his way. I would head for the lights of town. I hadn't walked very far when the car came creeping up beside me, with Chickie and her date in the front seat. Both of them implored me to get in. I didn't want to sit with Jim but I didn't want to walk back either so I climbed in beside Chickie in the front seat. All the way back to town Jim complained from the back seat and when they dropped me off, he said sarcastically, "See you at the prom."

The Korean College Student

I was thirteen years old. My older brother worked in an ice cream parlor. One day he told me that a Korean exchange student wanted to meet me. He had seen me in the ice cream store. I should go up to the store that evening. I did. I was introduced to the student who spoke extremely limited English. He indicated that he would like to walk on the nearby college campus where he attended college.

We strolled along, under the many trees, with me attempting to carry on a conversation. Suddenly the student hooked his leg around mine and tripped me. He came tumbling after and began his rough groping. I pushed him away and scrambled to my feet. I never saw him again nor did my brother ever mention him after I told him what the student had tried to do.

The Babysitter.

It was Autumn, I was fifteen years old and living back home and on probation. I always wanted to make money but the only thing I really knew how to do was baby-sit. One day I was with my friend Rosie and her brother who had taken his motorcycle to a repair shop. I was just standing around waiting for Rosie so we could go to the restaurant and listen to music. I noticed that the repairman was looking over at me quite a bit. Then he told Rosie's brother to wait just a minute. He walked over to where I was standing.

"Do you happen to baby-sit?" he asked me.

I told him yes. Then he said that he and his wife lived upstairs in the apartment above the shop. They had a little five year old boy. Would I be allowed to baby-sit for them, usually once a week? He would pick me up at my house and take me home afterwards. I told him yes.

I really liked his wife and their little boy. And they liked me. Maybe her husband had told her about the house by the railroad tracks where I lived. I think his wife felt sorry for me because one night close to Christmas when I was getting ready to be driven home, she handed me a big package, gaily wrapped in Christmas paper. She told me, "Merry Christmas!"

I unwrapped the present as soon as I got home. In it was a Western shirt and Western riding pants. The label said they were from a good company in Dallas. I tried them on and they fit perfectly. The next time I babysat, I thanked them for the generous gift. Soon after this I met the man I would marry and I didn't baby-sit so much.

Then one day in early February the man called and asked if I could baby-sit that night, that he and his wife had a special dinner they were to go to. I told him yes. I decided to wear the outfit they had given me for Christmas. He picked me up and drove us to the cycle shop. I climbed the stairs and he followed after.

"Is that the outfit Alma and I gave you?" he asked as we neared the top of the steps. I told him yes.

"Yes, I remember you told us you liked to ride horses."

I said that was true.

Inside the apartment I took off my pea jacket as his wife walked into the room.

"I just love this gift you gave me," I said as I turned around.

"Oh that is pretty on you!" she smiled.

I immediately started playing with little Billy. His mother told me to help myself to anything in the fridge and kitchen. Billy should go to bed at his usual bedtime and they would probably be home shortly after 10:00 p.m., which they were. I gave them the report on Billy and what a good little boy he always was. Then I got my jacket to get ready to leave. I said goodnight to the lady.

"I'll be home soon, Dear," the man told his wife.

I went down the stairs and started to open the door. The man's hand closed over mine on the handle. With his other hand he hit the light switch thereby plunging the whole shop into darkness. He put his arms around me and kissed me. I pushed him away.

"Shhh!" he whispered as I broke away from him.

I grabbed the doorknob and hurried out of the shop. He came after me.

"Sorry, I just got carried away. Don't worry, that won't happen again."

I wasn't so sure about that so I didn't baby-sit anymore for them. But a few weeks later, shortly before I was to get married, his wife called me and asked if I could sit? I told her I couldn't. I also told her I was going to get married soon and move away so I was sorry but I wouldn't be able to baby-sit in the future. I gave her the name of a friend of mine that she could call. Then she insisted on giving me a bridal shower. She called my friend and made all the arrangements. She invited several of my girlfriends on the next Saturday afternoon. There was cake and presents. She gave me a beautiful set of towels. I thought what a remarkable woman she was. I also wondered what would have happened to this wonderful woman if I hadn't been such a resistant babysitter?

The Pharmacist

This story has three forms of predation; Lurking, watching, waiting, attempting, rejection and then revenge. Watching and waiting. A short predation which ended with a wife who wrongly thought that I was having an affair with her husband and set out with a loaded gun to my workplace, intending to . . .

It was the first job I had after I left my husband. I was getting a welfare supplement but I wanted to work to make more money. I was hired as a clerk in a fancy "professional pharmacy." Many doctors and professional people frequented the store. I was hired, maybe because of my looks and personality. I showed the women how to better apply their makeup and sold quite a bit of it in the process.

One night after work the boss' wife called the pharmacy, looking for her husband. This was his usual night off. She was told, by the substitute pharmacist, who took my boss's place so he could go out with his friend, that her husband had gone out with me to have a drink.

I had agreed to go to meet a friend of my boss, a doctor who had asked him to introduce us and have a drink. I drove to the cocktail lounge, met the doctor, had a drink and left soon after. Maybe the boss used me as an alibi or maybe he thought we could double date later if the doctor and I hit it off.

It was the substitute's custom to work once a week for my boss, the pharmacist, so he could have a night off. I was used to men who came in the store, some of them friends of my boss, hitting on me. I dated a couple of them. So possibly the substitute thought I might be agreeable to going on a trip with him. This substitute was sixty-eight years old and about two weeks before the incident, had asked me to fly to Hawaii on the same plane that he and his wife were going to be on, (I would probably in economy while they were in first class) and then he would arrange to come and see me. He said he wanted to teach me how to work the stock market. I had politely refused. I thought of him as a Santa Clause, in fact he dressed as one at our Christmas party. He was old enough to be my grandfather. I declined.

This man was probably watching me while I worked. I was always pleasant to everyone. He was no doubt disgruntled by my turning him down on what he must have thought was a very generous offer. So when the boss's wife figured he was fooling around and asked the substitute that night where her husband was, he vindictively told her, 'With Christina.'

Anyway, regardless of what she imagined, I wasn't involved with him but somebody else was and I was the scapegoat. The wife came rushing into the pharmacy the next day, wildly brandishing a gun.

The boss waved his arms at me and yelled, "Hurry! Get out of here!"

I left. The boss called me later and told me I shouldn't come back in to work anymore, for my own safety.

I was completely innocent. I called the wife after that to tell her so, but she didn't believe me. I actually felt bad that she would think those things about me. I told her that I had a boyfriend and that I was practically engaged.

She said, " That wouldn't matter to a tramp like you!".

So that was it! No more job.

The Stranger On A Train

I was traveling on a train going back to Pittsburgh after a weekend in Indiana. Sitting in the club car and reading, I was aware when a man sat down in the chair next to mine. Soon he began a conversation, asking me where I was from and what I did there. He seemed friendly enough. He told me his name was Farouk. He said he was a filmmaker in Egypt. He was on his way to New York and then he would fly to California. He asked me if I had ever thought about a career in the movie industry. I laughed and told him no. He said he was impressed with my presence and he would like to call me in Pittsburgh, if he could have my phone number. I didn't think this would be risky so I gave it to him.

After a short while I grew sleepy so I told Farouk I was going back to my seat and try to take a nap.

I made my way through two cars and found my seat. I said good evening to the conductor then I settled into the seat and wrapped my jacket around me. I fell asleep but was wakened when I felt someone snuggling up to me and kissing me on the neck. It was Farouk.

"Stop that!"

I moved away from him but he persisted in pressing closer to me. I jumped up and headed for the door to go into the adjoining car. Then I saw the conductor and told him what had happened.

"Come with me," he said and motioned for me to follow him. He led me into another area and said that he would speak to the man and I shouldn't be bothered again.

And I wasn't bothered on the train. But two days after I returned home I got a phone call from Farouk. He said he was leaving New York and he would like to stop in Pittsburgh to see me and discuss a possible movie deal. I told him I didn't think that was a good idea. I wished him well and he did the same for me and I never heard from Farouk again.

END

Printed in the United States
By Bookmasters